Abyssinian Nomad

Maskarm Haile

Copyright © 2018 Maskarm Haile

All rights reserved.

ISBN-13: 9781775175704 (pbk.)
ISBN-13: 9781775175728 (hc.)

Disclaimer

The title of this book, *Abyssinian Nomad*, is to honor my Ethiopian heritage, since Abyssinia is what Ethiopia used to be called a long time ago. And most of my Ethiopian friends usually call me "Zelan" in Amharic, which means nomad.

To write *Abyssinian Nomad*, I relied significantly on my personal journal, mass emails I had sent out on my journey, couch requests I sent, my map, and my own memory of events.

I have changed the names of the people to protect their privacy, but all the stories I share in the book are based on my experience and true to me. I have omitted lots of names and stories just because it was hard to write only one book about a 9 month journey. But the omissions have no impact on the the substance nor the truth of the story.

The quotes and wiki references are from the internet—Thank you!

Contents

Introduction

Foreword 🚶 by Ffyona Campbell

Chapter 1 🦋 Growing Up

Chapter 2 🦋 The News that Shook My World

Chapter 3 🚶 Trust Your Dream;
　　　　　It Will Always Send You a Sign

Chapter 4 🚶 Cancer

Chapter 5 🦋 Gig in South Africa

Chapter 6 🚶 My On-and-Off Boyfriend

Chapter 7 ● Walking the Labyrinth

Chapter 8 🦋 Be Careful What You Wish For

Chapter 9 🎒 God Must Be Crazy

Chapter 10 🦋 Under the Clear African Sky

Chapter 11 🦋 The Smoke that Thunders

Chapter 12 🦋 The Poor Billionaire

Chapter 13 🌿 Lost in Translation

Chapter 14 🕯 Can We Pray For You?

Chapter 15 🦋 Badly proposed

Chapter 16 🦋 Chilling Truth

Chapter 17 🦋 The Biggest Loss of My Life

Chapter 18 🦋 Emerging from the Ashes

Chapter 19 🦋 But You Are Black

Chapter 20 🦋 Are You One of Us?

Chapter 21 🦋 The Man with an AK47 on the Bus

Chapter 22 🦋 The Spy with a Device

Chapter 23 🦋 Saved by the Brother

Chapter 24 🦋 Undercover Police

Chapter 25 🦋 Wait, Did I Just...

Introduction

"Your life is a sacred journey. And it is about change, growth, discovery, movement, transformation, continuously expanding your vision of what is possible, stretching your soul, learning to see clearly and deeply, listening to your intuition, taking courageous challenges at every step along the way. You are on the path... exactly where you are meant to be right now... And from here, you can only go forward, shaping your life story into a magnificent tale of triumph, of healing of courage, of beauty, of wisdom, of power, of dignity, and of love."
~ Caroline Adams

The book you are holding on your hand right now, didn't come easily for me. Giving birth to it has taken 9 years to be exact. It's irony, that a 9 month journey took 9 years to be written. It's not that I wrote the book for 9 years—I wish! I knew it was important to share this story with the world, and for years friends and strangers who heard my story suggested I should write a book. This put so much pressure on me; I spent the 8 years in deep fear, worrying, *How on earth I will be able to live up to the expectation?* I tried desperately to find a way to get out of it by finding other projects to throw myself into. But the voice within me that I mention in this book, it wouldn't stay silent, nor did anything I tried to do instead, give me any satisfaction or fulfillment.

I started out thinking I was going to write the book: "How to Backpack from Cape to Cairo as a Woman." But, whatever I wrote never felt right to my soul. My soul's desire to be truthful and to honor the personal physical, emotional, mental, and spiritual journey I had taken was strong. So strong that it never worked when I tried to write something else, in order to get out of reliving the emotions, and sharing my truth about my relationship with my mother, my loss, breakup, and some of the unpleasant experiences of my journey.

The actual writing of this book, took little more than a year. If I have to be honest and share that with you, it went like this:

60% of the time I was gripped in fear, feeling sick, and staring on my empty screen for hours, days at a stretch, and telling myself: *Who do I think I am to share my story? Why would anyone be interested in this?* And, *What a horrible writer I am,* (with lots of crying, drinking coffee, and eating chocolate).

10% of the time doing everything else except writing the book, even though I had decided to put my life on hold in every aspect in order to finish this book you are holding. (Still drinking more coffee and eating lots of sweets)

10% Rereading what I wrote and deleting. Rereading my journals from 9 years! Crying, writing, and sometimes sharing my work with a few people I trusted. Okay, actually there were only two people for long time. Still drinking more coffee, eating dessert, and wanting to die before pressing that send button with my writing attached.

20% Actual writing! This was when I sat without feeling time and space, unafraid, knowing and feeling it was my soul's purpose, and downloading from that place that I call my higher self. Each sentence or paragraph was accompanied with chills, a warm sensation in my entire body, smiles, and tears of joy that confirmed that, *I'm supposed to be doing what I'm doing, telling this important story that was bestowed on me.* In those magical moments the doubts, fear, questions, judgement, comparisons, and sadness has cleared and I'm just there as a medium rather than the person who is doing the work.

So, I can't claim this work as my own. If it were just me writing the book, you'd probably be holding a "how-to book" in your hand rather than a "travel memoir" that gives you a deeper understanding of where I come from: that explains why I travel so much, and what made my African journey so special and meaningful. In this book, you'll read why I'm so protective, unafraid, and unapologetic of my dream of traveling, and why I love, respect, and honor every experience, and every soul I cross paths with—because everything around my traveling is sacred and larger-than-life for me.

This writing, the writing of my truth, was done mostly at night, when everyone else had gone to sleep, and surprisingly, I didn't need coffee or sweets.

As I wrote my story from my heart, I realized that in my Africa journey I experienced the three stages of the Christian tradition of walking a labyrinth. Not only on the day I walked the beautiful labyrinth in the mountains of South Africa, but on my entire Africa journey. Africa was the labyrinth of my life. As I traveled, my burden of questions, fears, and grief increased until I reached the center of my labyrinth. It was at my lowest point of grief and sadness where I had no choice but to stop, reflect, and come to terms with what I'd experienced. Gradually, I was able to emerge from the ashes of my loss and learn to let go of the pain, and begin to understand the lesson that I was to learn in this labyrinth of a journey. I received hope and comfort from the beauty of nature and the connections with wonderful people I met along the way. I walked out of Africa feeling grounded, with new lessons, and a new perspective on life, ready to live my truth in this beautiful journey of life.

If you are one of those people who known me from my early childhood, I can't thank you enough for sticking around with me. Because I'm sure it wasn't easy sometimes.

If you are someone I met along my journey of travel, or work life, thank you for opening up to me, my crazy dream, and for listening to my endless travel stories.

If you just bought this book and we haven't crossed paths yet, I hope someday I meet you in person. Thank you for trusting me with your time and money to read this book, and I hope the story touches you in some way, and helps you in your own personal journey, whatever that may be.

Foreword

by Ffyona Campbell
author of On Foot Through Africa

As soon as I started reading *Abyssinian Nomad* I completely recognised Maskarm's spirit: an adventurous young woman with such a deep seated inner-strength that I knew it would see her through the many hardships and difficult life lessons of her journey.

When I read the part where she came across my book *On Foot Through Africa*, I completely understood how she had been inspired by it: it's as if our spirits had spoken to each other.

And I'm quite sure that this spirit will speak to you, through the pages of this book, and inspire all manner of adventures in your life too.

Happy days,

Ffyona Campbell

"All that I am or ever wanted to be, I owe to you, my angel mother."
~ *Abraham Lincoln*

To my mother

You loved me unconditionally and shared your love of life, and excitement for every experience, showing me the possibility of making everything graceful, whole-hearted and purpose-filled. You taught me to be open-minded, independent, to fight for what I believe in, and to never settle for less than my worth.

Without your love and trust I wouldn't be what I am today, nor the person I'm still working to become.
I miss you, but I know you are cheering from above.
I love you!

*Note that visited countries are marked in dark grey

Chapter 1: Growing Up

"Life shrinks or expands in proportion to one's courage."
~ Anaïs Nin

THE ETHIOPIAN STUDENTS IN MADRAS, India, had a tradition. When a new student came to join the college, they gathered together and took the student to the beach for their first-ever ocean experience. Coming from a landlocked country, the massive ocean was a wonder to our eyes.

When my turn came, I willingly and somewhat naively agreed to spend the evening at the beach with my new Ethiopian friends. They had invited some of their non-Ethiopian friends as well. We went to the beach as the sun was about to set and as the air began to cool down from the heat of the day. Seeing and smelling the ocean for the first time while walking on the fine, white sand, and then tasting the salt in my mouth before I even entered the water, made me giddy with happiness. While something within me danced for joy, there was a part of me that was terrified. I had never seen the ocean before and had no idea how to swim. I didn't feel prepared; I made a mental note that I needed to get a nice swimsuit and a towel.

Maskarm Haile

When everyone jumped into the waves, I stayed by the water's edge, hesitantly putting my feet in the water. And when I was least expecting it, a couple of students came up behind me, picked me up, and threw me into the waves.

That was my initiation. There was no time to think; I was in the middle of the waves trying to survive. My ears, nose, and mouth filled with the fine, white sand and salt water. I felt a mixture of bewilderment and unexpected exhilaration. Ever since that day, I have loved being in the ocean. Though I am still not a strong swimmer, I have learned to snorkel and scuba dive. Today one of my favorite things in the world is diving.

As I descend below the surface, I feel in complete harmony with everything. I am welcomed into a world of color, life and beauty. I experience the kind of peace one can only expect to feel with the freedom of weightlessness and nature's flow of life.

The sound of my own breathing slows my heart rate. The experience is rejuvenating, emotional, and spiritual as it fills me with gratitude, piques my curiosity, and allows me to get lost in that magical underwater world.

Until, suddenly, I wake up in a panic and look around, wanting my dive buddy or the dive master to hold my hand. I don't belong here!

Why am I telling you this? Because as my mother's first child and my parents' only child together, everything in my life has been trial and error. It feels as if I was thrown into this world without much guidance on how to survive. Millions of times, I have wished I had older siblings who could show me or tell me how to navigate through this thing called life. I have envied friends who have brothers or sisters that they looked up and wanted to emulate. At least those friends of mine didn't have to figure things out for themselves. They always had someone to ask and someone they could talk to.

Everything I did or wanted to do seemed to have consequences and risks.

Abyssinian Nomad

Being me never felt easy. In fact, my mother once said she could have raised three normal kids with the amount of energy, time, and money she invested in me. I was not sure what she meant by normal kids, but the truth was, *maybe she was right*. Offended, confused and worried about her comment, I suggested I should be given up for adoption or sent to boarding school. Even coming up with something like that was a shock to my long-suffering mother.

But no matter what I did, I always came back to my mother, seeking her guidance, love, and approval. She was always there, like my dive buddy or dive master, who I looked for to hold my hand when I was in the middle of a panic attack underwater.

I was trouble—even though I wasn't the typical rebellious teen experimenting with drugs and alcohol, I was the child who believed everything she read and heard. And that was a problem for my family. I read somewhere that children moved out of their parents' home when they were eighteen years old. So, at the tender age of twelve, I told my mother that "I am moving out when I turn eighteen."

I had pen pals in Sweden, Finland, Canada, the USA, and Italy. My mother had to help me write letters, and I used all my pocket money to send postcards, posters, and sometimes even Ethiopian souvenirs to friends I only knew by their photographs. In return, my mother used to bring home my mail, including boxes filled with color pens, patterned letter-writing pads with envelopes that made my heart melt, and some strawberry lip balm that smelled and tasted so sweet, my mother was afraid I might just eat the whole stick. My pen pals also introduced me to singers like Sting, Phil Collins, and Cindi Lauper; now and then I got a cassette tape or posters which I plastered on the walls in my bedroom.

I remember once sending my Finnish pen pal a family picture that was taken in our small garden while it was decorated for Christmas. She sent me, in response to seeing us having a sunny Christmas, my first-ever photo of snow. She explained how cold and dark it gets in Finland. Talk about a cultural shock for both of us, without even having left our respective countries.

I was also the kid who, before she even left school, sat down with college and university catalogs from around the world, and devotedly sent out requests for a scholarship before I had finished high school. Both to my family's surprise and mine, the colleges and universities sent me letters, and even more colorful catalogs that I poured over, dreaming about how wonderful it would be to study there.

My favorite game was to try to find the country and city of those colleges and universities on a map. And then finger walk the map while I daydreamt of studying there. I even sent a letter to the Vatican. Not only did they reply to my letter, but they also explained that there was no college or university in the Vatican City. I quickly looked for the Vatican on a map.

There was something else … My obsession with traveling and learning about the world started even earlier than my writing application letters. There has always been a voice inside me, for as long as I can remember. It is constant, scary, sometimes calming, curious, daring, loving, wired, encouraging, and forceful; it's a voice I fight with, try to reason with, argue with, am afraid of, but most of all I've learned to accept its existence. It's that voice that announced the earth-shattering inner knowingness—what I learned to call my big dream. The big dream was a very clear and profound awareness and desire to connect, learn and share with others traveling around the world. Although, as a child I didn't know how to express or articulate it, let alone how to make it happen.

That dream came to me when I was only five or six years old. My little body knew that the big dream was way bigger than me, bigger than my life! Every time I secretly thought about it, I felt a bolt of lightning through my body that excited and shocked my entire system and left me in awe and wonder. I thought that my big dream was some sort of sacred promise, maybe even a message from God himself. I knew I needed to keep my big dream a secret. Even though I was too young to wrap my head around it, I felt I'd been bestowed with something precious. When I think about all I've done in my life, one of the smartest things I believe I have done was not to tell a soul about my big dream. I didn't even mention it to my mother!

In my head, my big goal was very simple, or at least it sounded simple. But to put it into practice created problems. I didn't know anyone in my family or outside my family who talked about that kind of dream. The people I knew and the culture I grew up in only encouraged goals of becoming a doctor or an engineer or a lawyer. And the other major problem was that I was a girl—something my grandmother thought I needed to be reminded of daily.

When I was little, people asked, "Baby"—that was my nickname at home—"what do you want to be when you grow up?"

Me: "I want to become a lawyer so I can help women!"

And a few years later people said, "Baby, what do want to be when you grow up?"

Me: "I want to travel and help people."

I thought that might at least answer one of my big dreams. It was very vague, but it gave me the time I needed to own my big dream and keep it safe. It saved my family and teachers from panic. I contented myself by keeping my dream inside me, and it lived in my imagination. I fed it through the books I read, the art I saw, and the people I met. I occasionally escaped into my dream world when something happened that I didn't like.

Maskarm Haile

There was one more element that made my dream seem very wrong: I was growing up during the time of one of the most devastating famines in the history of the world. The one-channel TV and radio in Ethiopia talked about nothing but people dying of hunger. Though I was young and was not personally affected by it, I had witnessed how people were even afraid to talk about it. The images were horrifying, not only to children but to adults. It was a time of hopelessness and grief for most Ethiopians.

Like any kid growing up in the 80s, I was a big fan of Madonna, Michael Jackson, George Michael, Kenny Rogers—all the big names that played over and over on that one-channel TV and radio we had. And then United Support of Artists (USA) for Africa came to life.

"We are the world
We are the world, we are the children
We are the ones who make a brighter day
So, let's start giving
There's a choice we're making
We're saving our own lives
It's true we'll make a better day
Just you and me."

I played that song on the VHS again and again for years, as if there was a bigger message hidden in the most dramatic act of kindness I had witnessed in my short life. The whole setting and the story behind it had not only moved me, but had also put one of the biggest life questions in my heart.

"We are the world; we are the children...
There is a choice we are making,
We are saving our own lives..."

For years, I had appreciated strangers coming together to help Ethiopians. But I also wondered if what they were saying included me. "We are the world." Didn't that also include me? I didn't need to answer the next question—how is that you are saving your own life when you are helping millions of people to eat food and drink water? It took years more of life experience to understand what that small statement meant to me. But that song had given me what I needed and wanted: confirmation and a vision of myself as part of the world. Each time I listened to the music, I sang along with conviction, chanting to myself and whoever was listening. I didn't know all the words, but I knew the chorus very well. I also remember how the collective energy of those diverse artists made me feel when I was watching them on TV.

"We are the world." I am the world. I am part of the world. I knew there was a bigger picture, though at that stage I had no words to articulate and communicate it. But I knew deep in my heart how it felt. I was not crazy after all. I was not alone in this. *Or was I?* Armed with the awareness that I was not alone, and my secret dream, I continued to live my day-to-day life. I would like to think I had a very normal upbringing for a child who was born in a middle-class Ethiopian family. There was nothing extraordinary about my family or me. Education was important; there was no other way.

I spent most of my early childhood with my grandparents (at one stage I thought they were my biological parents and that my mother was my big sister). My mother used to work a lot. And it didn't take long to realize that my grandmother was very concerned about me.

According to my grandmother, I was a very bubbly, happy, and fat baby with lots of jet-black curly hair who enjoyed being taken and kissed by everyone and didn't fuss. As I grew, my affectionate nature started to break traditions the elders had about hugging and kissing children. I didn't seem to outgrow the desire for affection. My grandmother was also concerned about the way I walked around the house. She said I walked looking at the sky or at people's eyes. But as a girl, and even as a woman, I was supposed to look down. I also knocked into things with my long legs, as I wasn't paying attention to where I was going. I wasn't always aware of what was happening around me.

She worried about how much I loved anything with wheels that moved quickly—cars, taxis, buses and big trucks. She worried about my love for chocolate and sweets. She worried about my lack of interest in domestic work (cooking, cleaning, making coffee) and the disasters I created in the kitchen.

Emaye, as I called my grandmother, worried about who would want to marry me. She was also deeply concerned about my love and trust for people, and she worried about by my tendency to get lost in my own world. And most of all, she worried about my asking, "Why?" more often than anyone could answer.

My relationship with my mother, on the other hand, wasn't easy or straightforward. It took a long time to accept her as my mother, since I was spending a lot of my time with my grandparents while she was away most of the time, traveling for work. But still, I knew my connection to her was very strong. When asked who my hero was, I would always answer, "My mother." She was my greatest inspiration and larger than life itself to me; I worshiped the ground she walked on.

Even as a child, when I saw my mother, I could tell that she was different. Different from her mother, from the cousins around us. She didn't live her life as most women were expected to live in Ethiopia in the 1970s. She had a job, so I hardly saw her at home while I was growing up. My upbringing taught me that there were women like my grandmother and there were women like my mother—a woman did not have to fit one specific mold; she could be whoever she wanted to be.

My mother worked as a humanitarian aid worker with the United Nations, traveling to respond to the famine in Ethiopia. Later, she worked with women and babies in and around rural Ethiopia. All I wanted to become was my mother—strong, independent, loved, and respected by others. Most of all, I wanted to travel and make a difference in people's lives. However, I didn't want to have kids as my mother had. I felt she gave up so much because of us.

Having a strong mother taught me the value of independence and taking responsibility for my life. I don't have a favorite meal my mother cooked and I now crave. In fact, I hardly saw my mother in the kitchen growing up. But she showed me how to do things with grace and walk with my head held high. She taught me that I needed to know "why" and the importance of faith. That I should learn to embrace change, and to realize that the world doesn't revolve around me—which taught me about being open.

By working, my mother showed me that my big dream was possible. But my big dream differed from my mother's in one critical way. I wanted to travel the world, meeting people while changing lives. She opted to have family and stay in one place. And then in my late twenties, when she saw the direction I was taking my life, she was extremely unhappy. It was clear from her office photo board, things had gone as planned for my mom until I had graduated from college with my BA in Economics. But after that, the photos on her board didn't convey the same message as her colleagues'. She had a picture of me jumping out of a plane, standing near the Eiffel Tower, swimming with a polar bear, or carrying a backpack while traveling, while her friends had pictures of their children's weddings and grandchildren.

I saw her doubt herself for the first time. She blamed herself for the freedom she gave me to choose. Like many other women, she blamed herself for who her children became. Genuinely confused, she asked me what I was running away from. It was then I saw that this most understanding, open, and strong woman—my mother—wasn't all that strong after all. Her desire for me to succeed in the traditional sense, to have a family, was so strong that, to my horror, her disapproval of my chosen life threatened to take away every value she had instilled within me.

The result was for the first time in my life, I doubted myself.

But no matter how much I doubted myself, I loved my mother. I trusted her words. Her feelings mattered so much to me that I was willing to give in to her desires… most of the time.

Then the unthinkable happened.

My mother was diagnosed with breast cancer.

Chapter 2: The News that Shook My World

*"One is never afraid of the unknown;
one is afraid of the known coming to an end."*
~ Jiddu Krishnamurti

I HAVE IMAGINED LOTS OF THINGS in my life, but this… never!!

On September 23, 2004, I went out for a long walk on my lunch break to enjoy the crisp September air and the burst of fall color in old Montreal. I was working a nine-to-five job in finance, which I had taken to pay my bills and feed my travel appetite. I loved the change of season, and my calendar was filled with fall activities I planned to do on weeknights and weekends. On my walk, I was just debating whether to go hiking or apple picking with a group of friends, or maybe organize that last picnic in the park before the sun was replaced with snow.

With that in mind, I arrived back at work.

There was a random email from my mother. At least, that's what I thought it was when I saw the subject "Email" appear in my work inbox. Perhaps it would be a reply to the long email I had sent to her. I was quick to drop everything and started reading with excitement. Two days earlier, I had spoken to my mother about a work trip she was planning to take to South Africa from Ethiopia. And without any suspicion, I was marveling about her visit to that fascinating country that I, too, dreamed of visiting one day. I had promised to call her once she was there, thinking how wonderful it would be to dial a new country code.

My mother started by thanking me for my last email. Next, she let me know that she had reached Johannesburg safely and that she needed to be on medication for longer than she had anticipated. And then she said, "Sorry for the bad news, can you call me on the following number?" Her sentences were all over the place, mostly misspelled and with the sorts of typos you only make when you are in shock or in a hurry. Deep inside, I started to tremble. It was as if my body knew a secret that my brain, or even my heart, refused to acknowledge. Hands shaking, I dialed the number my mother had emailed. I felt a heaviness. I could hardly move my body. A feeling of numbness and panic took over my body and mind. My eyes filled with tears. But why? She only said she needed medication. The question was, for what?

I looked around, wondering how my world could change so fast. A few minutes ago, my challenge was trying to decide whether to go hiking or apple picking, and now...

Everything seemed normal in the office; all my coworkers glued to their computers.

I tried the number my mother gave me, but no one answered, since unbeknownst to me, it was not her room number. I redialed and redialed the number, until, finally, someone answered and transferred my call to my mother's room. At that point, I was crying in a full-blown, ugly way in my office. I didn't care. I wanted my mom, and I was thousands of miles away from her. Her email had said there was bad news. My mother was not a woman who talked about bad news over emails or phone calls. Sometimes it would be years before I found out when someone got sick or passed on in the family. I was shaking and crying uncontrollably when she finally picked up the phone and said my name.

My mom tried to console me, saying it was nothing, that she would be okay once she had gotten the medication, and that I had nothing to worry about, as she was surrounded by great doctors who knew what they were doing. And everything was covered by her insurance. I was desperate to believe her, but for the first time in my life I heard my mother's voice shaking. I heard fear and uncertainty, as though even she didn't believe what she was saying. Between sobs, I asked what her diagnosis was. She went silent. I was silent, too, because I didn't even want to breathe fearing I might miss the word she was about to say. In that moment of stillness, I heard a voice within myself, my intuition, say, *"Cancer. Breast cancer."*

I buried my head on my office desk and cried some more as I heard my mother saying that the doctors were still doing some tests. Maybe she said more, but I was not listening. My colleagues started circulating my cubicle. Although they had no idea who I had been talking to, they overheard words like "treatment, doctors, and diagnosis."

I never heard the word "cancer" from my mother's mouth. But I shouted the word in my head: *"CANCER? CANCER!"* I suddenly felt overwhelming guilt with the fear. *How could I even think my mother would have cancer? Why would anything like that even have crossed my mind? Cancer? There was cancer in Ethiopia?* I remembered all the movies I watched growing up and crying my eyes out when a woman was diagnosed with this thing called cancer. Most of these movies showed how a woman struggled and fought for her life before dying, leaving her husband and kids behind. Though I had come a long way, and had a little more awareness about cancer in general, I had never known anyone who was affected by the disease in Ethiopia. I didn't even know it existed in Ethiopia and if it did, I wasn't sure what it was called in Amharic, an Ethiopian language. And not knowing it made me feel even more guilty, because I felt that I had wished that horrible thing, which didn't exist in her culture, on my mother.

I breathed in, trying to follow what my mother was telling me. The doctors were doing tests; she would soon know the diagnosis. But it didn't make sense—if the doctor already knew she needed long treatment, how did they not know the diagnosis? *Not knowing sounded more hopeful,* I told myself.

Minutes later, I called my sister in Ethiopia, and she broke it down for me. "Our mother has been diagnosed with breast cancer, and the doctors have suggested she start chemotherapy immediately."

Though the journey was hard, and she was separate from her family and friends in Ethiopia, my mother's body responded well to the treatment. We all rallied around to support her in every way possible, which helped her as well. To my surprise, there were other Ethiopian women with her in South Africa, getting cancer treatment at the same time. Most of them were evacuated by the UN because either they or their husbands worked for the UN.

~~~

Fast-forward three years later to 2007, and my mom was given the "all clear" by doctors in South Africa. Not only was she back in Ethiopia, but she went back to work too. We all felt relieved; the difficult time was behind us now.

Then I got an email that said, "Call me, I'm in South Africa." The last time I'd seen my mother was a year earlier. I had spent a few days in Addis Ababa, Ethiopia, before I embarked on my adventure in Australia. That visit didn't go very well, as we both had different agendas. All I wanted to do was spend some time with her. But for her, it was an opportunity to hook me up again with my ex-boyfriend, a man my family loved and respected. Now, with "cancer" a word of our past, I thought the phone call was going to be another dreaded conversation about my unmarried and childless life and her desire to fix that. Though I didn't want to have that conversation again, I was happy my mother was in a country where I could call her and have a long, uninterrupted conversation. Calling Ethiopia isn't a pleasant thing to do; the connections are terrible, and there is a good chance of simply not being able to hear each other.

I waited for the right time to call. I was in Australia, and she was in Pretoria, South Africa, with a time difference of nine hours. When we got a chance to talk, my mother started with her typical, long, never-ending greeting and asked about my trip. She sounded calm and almost happy about what I was doing. I was a little impatient. I have always felt that the long, never-ending greetings are a way of avoiding meaningful sharing, and I resent that part of the Ethiopian culture. So, I casually asked why she was back in South Africa. Suddenly, she sounded too tired to talk and passed the phone to my younger sister, who was with her. Once again, my sister had to break it down for me: the cancer was back, and it had started to spread. The doctors had already started my mother on another round of chemotherapy, and it was expected to be a long journey. The phone call was to ask me if I could go back to South Africa to be with her since my sister had to go back to work.

Nothing made sense. Everything went dark around me, and I heard myself saying, "But how? Didn't they clear her, saying she's free of cancer?" My mother had even gone back to work. *Did the doctors miss something the first time around?* I was at a loss for words. My sister asked me again when I could be in Pretoria.

I felt life was being unfair and cruel to my mother. I knew her desire to live and her long "to-do" list. Life wasn't giving her a chance; she needed to get a break. She deserved to be healthy and happy after what she had already gone through. It was a total blow. I wondered how she was taking the news. I ached for her, for the dreams she had to put on hold, once again, until she finished her treatment.

I was in Australia, on a trip that had started as a short, five-week journey around the country, but had turned into a one-year adventure. Armed with a six-month working holiday visa and a ticket to Japan, I was on my way to Tokyo, to arrive in time to attend my best friend's wedding. But with news like that, the decision was quick and straightforward. I bought a one-way ticket to Johannesburg.

Chapter 3: Trust Your Dream; It Will Always Send You a Sign

*"To Everyone else it looked like a single leap,
But in reality it was hundreds of Little Baby Steps."
~ Rebecca Campbell*

I WOULDN'T BE EXAGGERATING IF I say reading books has saved my life.

When I am happy,
I read,
When I am sad, confused, lost,
I read,
When I need information, want to learn something new,
I read,
I read everywhere and all the time…

My on-and-off then-boyfriend Brian had come to meet up with me and travel through part of Australia just before I found out my mother's illness had returned. It was our last weekend in Australia when we decided to visit the Sunday Port Douglas farmers' market. We both had a thing for strolling around farmers' markets and trying different local products. But what made that particular market meaningful for me was the table of second-hand books. To me, a farmer's market with used books and great coffee is heaven.

At the second-hand bookstall, I walked around the table reading the titles, touching and feeling the books and magazines. There is a comfort that comes from being around and holding books. I also have a theory that second-hand bookstore owners are not in the business for the money: they love books and are rare human beings who rescue used books and find them suitable homes.

There is something else that happens when I pick up a second-hand book and hold it: I long for the story of the person who had just read the book. How did it change their lives? Did it make them laugh? Where were they when they were reading it? I have found a boarding pass used as a page marker, something I often do. I can imagine finding all those people to tell them I'm reading the very same book they read once. I think about asking them where they were when they read the book, to see if our lives were somehow in the same place when we read that particular book.

That day at the farmers' market, one book caught my eye. It was in a box for much older books, and I immediately picked it up and held it close to my heart. The book had a picture of a blonde girl in simple white shorts and a blue and white T-shirt. Her skin looked as tanned as the red grass behind her, and she carried a long stick the same way the young African villagers did as they walked. The title read: *On Foot through Africa*, by Ffyona Campbell.

I was instantly drawn to her, to the book, and there was a knowingness that took place in my heart and soul. I felt my heart warming as if I were reconnected with a long-lost friend or family member, who was looking directly at me and whispering, "If I can do it, so can you!"

Two thoughts crossed my mind at that moment. First, a great relief to know that I was not crazy, and then the realization that someone else has been living my dream. I bought the book and walked away knowing exactly what I was going to do with it. That book was going to be my travel companion for my long flight, from Melbourne, Australia, to Johannesburg, South Africa.

I read the book fast, as if my life depended on it! In a way, I guess it did. I mean, if a white woman from the UK could cross Africa by foot, how hard could it be for an African woman like me to do it? I kept thinking that my African background and my skin color would give me leverage, that I would be able to slip past the borders without actually creating attention. While reading the book I felt my excitement rising, my heartbeat racing. It was one of the most intense books I'd ever read. I was fascinated and inspired by Ffyona's courage. But it was also unfortunate to learn she had to be evacuated twice because of war, and children throwing stones at her. I knew there were still some countries in Africa that were so unpredictable when it comes to war. Yet despite the dangers, it was as if all I had needed was someone's permission to achieve my dream of crossing Africa and meeting people while experiencing our culture and seeing the natural beauty of the land. With every sentence Ffyona had written, she was releasing me. Once again, the voice within me spoke, loud and clear. It was time!

As George Kimble said, "The darkest thing about Africa has always been our ignorance of it." To most people, even today, Africa seems like one country. It's generally labeled as dangerous, untamed, and unknown, so therefore petrifying. But traveling in Africa was anything but monolithic.

In my experience, traveling in Africa was the most rewarding adventure I'd ever undertaken. For a travel addict like me, who challenges the norm and explores off of the

Maskarm Haile

beaten track, there was a lifelong lesson that came with my journey. If it is given the opportunity, Africa will crack your heart open and make space for something different, a wild and unbelievably magical experience. Traveling in Africa can also give the opportunity not only to visit some amazing wildlife and vast deserts, but also to make a difference in people's lives. It could bring out the best in people, or the worst.

Chapter 4: Cancer

*"When it rains, look for rainbows.
When it's dark, look for stars."*
~ Oscar Wilde

IT WAS A VERY EMOTIONAL reunion with my mother. I had asked her not to come to the airport to pick me up, but she was there when I arrived. She looked tired and fragile. I only knew what my sister had told me, that she needed two rounds of chemotherapy, which might take about a year. I didn't dare to ask my mother for more information, and she was not volunteering any.

This is it, I told myself. *The roles have reversed and I am here to take care of my mother.*

But I didn't want to only accompany my mother to doctor appointments and chemotherapy sessions. I wanted to do more for my mother, and for me—because she wasn't alone in this journey. But in a silent culture like ours, where the rule seems to be to hide the illness to the grave, where should I begin? How could I know what she needed? What she wanted? Or felt?

Maskarm Haile

But there was one thing I knew about my mother: *She has zest for life and she is a fighter.* I knew this wasn't a battle she'd easily lose. I told myself my job was to be there, and to fight with her. Support her in everything I could and make sure the journey was worthwhile.

My mother was staying at a guesthouse in Pretoria. A young and vibrant Ethiopian couple with a beautiful newborn son ran the guesthouse. The place was cozy, with bright, big, sunlit rooms and a pool at the back. The welcoming environment, having other Ethiopians drop by for a visit or stay, the Ethiopian decoration on the walls, and the occasional Ethiopian food makes the guests feel more like they're at home in Ethiopia. When I arrived, the owners were treating my mother as their own family, and it was easy for me to fit in and feel at home.

But there was nothing that prepared me for accompanying my mother to her chemotherapy. Though my mom knew what to expect and she'd been going for weeks before I got there, it was my first time, and I was clueless. I spent a sleepless night worrying and trying to convince myself I could do this. But when I woke up, I felt and looked sicker than my mother. Paralyzed with fear, I ran into the bathroom feeling nauseated before my mom could see me and ask questions. Just thinking about seeing my mother in a chair or bed with needles stuck in her body made me want to run away from everything.

I cried enough in the shower, and made sure there was nothing in my stomach before going to the hospital. I carried water bottles and energy drinks for both of us, wore my brave face, and stood outside in the sun waiting for my mother and the driver to take us to the hospital.

I clutched my mother's hand in the car, not knowing what to say, only feeling the dense air in the car. My mother introduced me proudly to Bongani, the UN driver who came to take her to her appointment. I chatted half-heartedly with him about the meaning of our names, still holding tight to my mom's hand and looking out the window from the back seat, until he told me his name means "Be Thankful." I sat straight up, feeling the words putting me back in my body.

Be Thankful, I repeated the words in my mind. The truth was I needed to be thankful for being able to be with my mother, for her to have the opportunity to get treatment. At the time of my mother's cancer journey, there was only one oncologist, Dr. Bogale Solomon, for more than eighty million people in Ethiopia.[1] My mother was one of his outpatients when she was in Ethiopia. Not many people had the opportunity my mother received to get medical evacuation and be treated by highly qualified professionals in a clean, pleasant, and peaceful environment like this.

~~~

Driving to Johannesburg from Pretoria felt very long, but once we arrived, I saw how my mother was a familiar face to most of the nurses who came to greet her and ask her how she was doing. She proudly introduced me to each and every one of them, the kind people who took their time to say hello. She also knew some of the patients who were sitting around getting their chemo. It was a kind of family gathering, mostly women, all sitting in big reclining chairs, some chatting with one another, some chatting with the people accompanying them.

---

[1] According to Dr. Yohannes Woldeanuel, Ethiopia has a population of more than eighty-four million people and is expected to become the ninth most populous country in the world by 2050. The growing population coupled with lifestyle changes will mean an increasing burden of cancer. However, oncology services are wholly inadequate — no cancer registry exists, and only one cancer center, with a handful of doctors and nurses, struggles to serve the entire country. Black Lion Hospital, Addis Ababa, houses Ethiopia's only cancer referral center.
https://www.researchgate.net/publication/236126483_Cancer_in_Ethiopia

Maskarm Haile

It was hard to witness my mother's pain, as the friendly nurse came first to take blood to make sure her white blood cell count was stable before she administered the chemo through an IV my mother's arm. Needles have always bothered me, either watching someone receive an injection, or getting one myself. But it broke my heart seeing my mother close her eyes both with pain and from not wanting to see the needle.

She tried to stay cheerful even though it was clear she was in pain. I sat on the floor massaging her feet, wishing to take away the pain. Now and then the nurse came around with lollipops, checking on the patients and lightening the room with some joke. I was touched to see no matter what was going on, everyone said hello, smiling when someone arrived, and said goodbye when they left. They wished each other well, and showed courage and calm. With cancer, unlikely bonds are formed, transcending age, race and gender.

After coming back from chemotherapy that day, seeing my mother in pain lying on the bed made me realize, though it was hard, how lucky I was to be given that time with her. It could be an opportunity and blessing if we used the time. I had a lot to work on; there was a lot to say to my mother, and I hoped she too would be open to say her piece.

When my mother was diagnosed in 2004, I had turned to the online community where caregivers (families) discuss their journey, and I also read the spiritual teacher Louise Hay's books for comfort and guidance. One of the things I repeatedly heard that resonated with me was working toward forgiveness. And I knew that was very important for me and my mother. But when was a good time to bring up those heavy family subjects?

The next few months, in between chemotherapy treatments, I had the chance to introduce my lifestyle to my mother through couchsurfers, both travelers and locals. Initially, she blamed and doubted herself for the way I turned out, but over the months I saw my mother ease into understanding that I was not the only one with a lust for travel. She had felt that she was the only mother who carried the burden of an unmarried daughter, a daughter who wanted to wander the world without the prospect of leaving a legacy through bringing a child into the world. But, thanks to couchsurfing coffee or drink meetups, she met and spoke to numerous young, and not so young, people about a lifestyle she never could have imagined. My mother found it interesting how articulate, open, and honest we couchsurfers were about our feelings. She was surprised at how much we trusted each other with our dreams, emotions, and desires and were able to share at that level. She had never experienced that, ever! Her generation and the ones before never sat around with strangers discussing their personal lives.

It was new to her, magical, and at the same time, scary. Through those couchsurfing brunches, lunches, dinners, picnics, and drinking sessions, my mother not only discovered a new world, but also found her daughter. She heard my stories with strangers, heard about my fears, desires, challenges, goals, and aspirations. I sometimes saw a touch of sadness in her eyes. I wondered if that sadness was regret about something, or worry about her own life? In those couchsurfing meetings, there was no limit to the subjects we discussed. The topics ranged from trying to find love, to breakups and broken marriages, to LGBTQ rights, spirituality, women's struggles with wanting to have children (freezing eggs, sperm donation), loss of loved ones...

Before those meetings, my mother had had no idea where I stood on most of those issues.

And I absolutely had no idea, when my friend Tascha asked my mom what she considered her greatest achievement in her life, that she would say her children. *What?* I don't know about my sisters, but I had spent most of my life believing my mother would have done much better if she didn't have kids.

Despite all that new openness, I still wasn't able to tell her I had broken up with Brian. I was afraid she would be disappointed and worried about me. That was a secret my friends and I had to keep when she was around.

I also had the chance to spend time with her friends, mostly the UN expats based in South Africa. They gave me the opportunity to learn so much more about my mom's generation and also about Ethiopia as a country. When they talked about Ethiopia, I always felt like it wasn't the same country I grew up in; they grew up in a different era when there was still a king, Haile Selassie I, when education was valued and serving the country was considered an honor. There were times I wished I had been born then: it felt like they had vision, understanding, and a sense of responsibility for their country.

When my mother and I were alone in the guesthouse, to get my mother's mind off the chemotherapy, hospital trips, and anything that involved medicine, I tried to keep her busy by sharing pictures and stories of my travel. Though she didn't approve of my hitchhiking or staying with strangers, the mood was quite light, and we laughed about the stories most of the time. When I mentioned *On Foot through Africa*, I couldn't control the intensity of my attraction to the story. It was clear that she didn't like the story or the way I was talking about it.

It was as if her motherly instinct had informed her where I was going with that.

My mother was not ready to go. I knew that for a fact because she didn't even like to talk about other people's deaths, let alone her own. I am not afraid of my own death, maybe because I have lived my life on the edge. My life has always felt like a huge roller-coaster ride. If there is one thing I've learned from that, it's an awareness of my mortality. I know I cannot be afraid of dying, and I wanted to cross Africa despite the risks. So, I had made peace with my death a long time ago. But the thought of death was not the same when I thought of the possibility of losing my mother so soon. It was something that had never even crossed my mind until then, and it terrified me. She lived a passion- and purpose-driven life, more than most people I had ever known. She also secretly wanted to retire early from her job to raise at least one grandchild, and hoped that one of her children would finally fulfill her dream. I was her weird child, who engaged in conversations not only about death, but about life after death, reincarnation, and connecting with the spirit world.

She always listened to what I had to say but never encouraged or discouraged me. Our conversations were dominated by her wishes, and I secretly hoped one of my sisters would make her dream come true, knowing deep inside me that I would do anything for my mother except that. We had been discussing her desire for a grandchild for a long time, and she kept bringing the subject up, hoping for a miracle and my change of heart.

I knew what she wanted. I also knew then that we were not lucky enough to have what she wanted, but we could make the best of what we had. My mother had amazing friends who understood her situation and made sure she felt loved and taken care of in every way. So, with everyone's help, we focused on using the time; we traveled to the national wildlife parks between chemotherapy, hung out with friends and went to spas. Most of all, we talked. I spoke most of the time; I wanted to make sure my mother understood me, accepted me for who I was. After all, I had spent most of my life trying to get her attention, approval, acceptance, and love.

While all that was going on, my mother's health wasn't getting any better. The chemotherapy was eating up her body, and she was getting weak and was often tired. We were spending more time at home and less time going out to the malls and cafes and meeting with her friends.

One morning, we were at the hospital for her regular checkup with her doctor. He looked disturbed and extra cautious as he welcomed us into his office. I was worried, as I was the only family member there with her. The doctor told us in the gentlest way possible that it would be better if she were to go back home to rest a bit, since her body couldn't take the chemotherapy anymore, or something to that effect. I couldn't understand what he was saying because everything went dark and silent. Suddenly, I felt chills engulf my body. To avoid passing out, I tried to find a focus point, so I stared at a wall behind the doctor. I wasn't looking at him anymore or listening to what he was saying. But I kept reminding myself that I couldn't pass out—I still needed to help my mother back to the car.

The moment passed... I didn't feel like I was going to faint anymore, but my body seemed to have given up as my eyes filled with tears. I avoided looking at my mother or the doctor. He was still talking. I wondered if I was supposed to say something, but nothing came out of my mouth. My mother listened quietly, nodding her head politely.

All I could think was, *I wish I knew what she is thinking*.

The doctor was professional, saying things about the medication she could take. I finally interrupted the conversation and said, "Rest? For how long?" I shot a pleading look at the doctor, hoping that he was not giving up on my mother! He looked at me with compassion, but I once again avoided looking at him or my mother, and waited for his voice. I needed to hear that I had just imagined the worst and everything would be okay again. It was not what I heard; I listened to a shaky voice similar to how my mother sounded the first time she called me from South Africa. There was no confidence in his words; he was not sure. It was not what he said, but what I was hearing and feeling.

That doctor, whom I had literally worshiped to help create a miracle to save my mother, wasn't confident. As much as I sensed his compassion, I wanted him to be egoistical and tell me that there was nothing he couldn't fix. But none of that happened. He just responded by saying she should rest as much as she needed. He was going to transfer her file to the doctor in Ethiopia. Once again, I reminded myself there was no time for tears; my mother needed me. So I summoned up my courage and said to her, "It's good. You will get a little break from this and go home for few weeks." I don't remember much else, but I blabbered as we walked to the car, tightly holding each other's hands.

Chapter 5: Small Gig in South Africa

"Not everything is supposed to become something beautiful and long-lasting"
~ Emery Allen

MY MOTHER REFUSED MY OFFER to accompany her to Addis Ababa, Ethiopia, saying I should stay in South Africa. The reason was clear: a few weeks before the news about her going back, I had started a small gig with APRM (African Peer Review Mechanism) as a Finance & Administration Consultant to keep me busy and pay my bills. APRM is a self-monitoring instrument voluntarily agreed to by member states of the African Union. At the time I joined the office, it had twenty-five member states. The chairperson was the late Melese Zenawi, Prime Minster of Ethiopia, and the panel members included Prof. Adbayo Adedeji, from Nigeria, Amb. Bethel Kiplagat from Kenya, Prof. Dorothy Njeuma from Cameroon, Prof. Mohammed Seghir Babés from Algeria, Dr. Graça Machel (the late Nelson Mandela's wife) representing Mozambique, Mme. Marie-Angélique Savané from Senegal, and Dr. Chris Stals, from South Africa. All were from Africa's elite; names I grew up hearing.

Finding myself in one room with them was a surreal and magical experience that I will never forget. In fact, I had practiced my introduction to Dr. Graça Machel way ahead of our meeting, only to forget everything when I stood in front of her and simply babbled. She got up from her seat and gave me a hug. I had been a fan of her and Nelson Mandela. Being in the presence of these leaders was inspiring and overwhelming to say the least.

Though I knew the experience was going to be short-lived, I put every ounce of my energy into the work I was doing, never taking the opportunity for granted. It felt like a perfect sign that I should pursue my dream of crossing Africa, as it provided the little cash I needed.

For my mother, that small gig was a mini-miracle that she thought would change my life and mind and lead me to settling down somewhere in Africa.

After my mother left, I was feeling angry, bitter, confused, and very sad, not only about how everything was unfolding for my mother, but for our family too. Our mother was the rock for everyone who glued the family together. Without her, it was clear everything would fall apart.

I decided all I wanted and needed was to throw myself into something bigger than me, something that would take away my fear and pain, channel my energy into something positive. I needed to do something that would either give me faith about life, or kill me in the process of trying to do it and get me out of my misery.

I mastered the courage to tell my mother that I wanted to start my journey through Africa, since I was already in South Africa.

Convincing my mother wasn't easy. I solicited her trusted friend, Israel, to help me convince her that it would be a good idea for me to stay in Africa. I even told her, since I would be traveling north, that I would spend time with her when I got to

Maskarm Haile

Addis Ababa. I also told her that I would be close if, God forbid, she needed me to fly to Addis to be with her. I begged her to be more honest with me when I called, and I promised to fly to see her in Ethiopia before my travels took me there if she wanted me to. And she agreed! With fear and tears in her eyes, she gave me her blessing for my journey. Now there was no other option for me but to embark on my unknown voyage.

I told myself: *If Africa doesn't kill me, I know it will heal me.*

I was quick to start getting organized for my trip. My mom's friend Israel had given me the big Lonely Planet Africa guidebook and *Dark Star Safari*, by Paul Theroux for my birthday, which I read religiously and made notes for myself. I also sent couch requests and looked for traveling tips and any important information for the places I'd be visiting. There was one problem with couch requests, though: I had no idea when I was going to be in the cities, towns, or villages. Everything was open and depended on how long my bus and taxi trips would take and the amount of time I would spend in each country. (Back then, couchsurfing wasn't very popular. And to my mother's horror, I was an official couchsurfing ambassador.) The response was incredible; at least people wanted to meet me for coffee or sightseeing. Most couchsurfers who were able to host were expats—the locals mostly lived with their families and didn't have extra space, but they offered whatever they could.

It was very encouraging to have people to visit in most places. I thought it would make my traveling a little easier. I was also secretly hoping to find people like me, passionate African travelers. Thanks to couchsurfing, I have come across hundreds of travelers, nomads from all around the world, but not one African yet. I was hoping that even if they were not traveling, I would find my tribe in Africa. My other secret desire was to be considered normal in the eyes of other Africans, my family, and African friends, because most of my conversations end with a sentence like, "You are different!" I also had one bigger hidden desire—to prove to my mother that there are other young Africans like me, so she wouldn't feel bad about what I was doing.

Brian and I talked often, even though my mother had gone back to Ethiopia and he didn't have to call me anymore. But we kept on communicating with each other, which bewildered my friends.

It seemed natural to me, after all, he was the one person I could say anything to, and he was also my emergency contact. I did not fully share my desire with everyone to cross war-torn countries, but Brian knew about it. One day he called me out of the blue, to ask a question that stunned me. He asked, "Aren't you afraid of anything?" He couldn't understand how I could seem so fearless. I had to answer him—he sounded a little irritated—and I needed to come up with something brilliant, something that showed my vulnerability and bravery at the same time. And I found it; I had the answer, and for a moment I was very proud of myself. I also felt relieved to be able to answer on the spot, since I hadn't taken the time or luxury to think about what I'm afraid of before. I'd had such big things on my mind, like traveling, and now, losing my mother.

So I proudly said I was afraid of things that crawl.

Quickly drafting a mental note for myself to make sure my sleeping bag would close properly, I heard a surprised voice that was even more irritated by my answer. I was quite impressed with myself, but I guessed he wasn't. He said, "You want to backpack in one of the most dangerous parts of the world, and your fear is just crawling insects?" The truth was some of my friends had graphically explained all the possible things that could happen to me, like getting raped, mugged, kidnapped, being attacked by wildlife, or killed. But I never cared to internalize their warnings or even entertain the possibility of any of it happening. I had my list of worries when I thought of crossing Africa, but didn't have any real fears. My list was of things like finding a clean bathroom, getting my period on the road, and finding fresh water.

Then Brian called me again, to announce that he was planning to join me.

Chapter 6: On-and-Off Boyfriend

"It is difficult to know at what moment love begins; it is less difficult to know that is has begun."
~ Henry Wadsworth Longfellow

I ALMOST FROZE WHEN BRIAN announced he was coming to join me. You would think I would feel relief or excitement. No! I felt anger, intense anger! My mind flooded with thoughts.

I felt betrayed because the one person who I thought understood me, and believed in me and my travel, was questioning me. If he thought I could do this on my own, he wouldn't want to come with me. *Or would he?*

Usually, when I get angry, I lose all my words and shut down inside, but not that day. I wanted answers, not only from Brian, but from within myself. All the fear and doubt that was wrapped around this trip from family and friends had slowly begun to creep in, and it felt like I was going to lose my own ground.

I panicked, but still asked him why he wanted to come with me. Did he feel the need to save the African girl from Africans?

Maskarm Haile

He paused.

He wasn't fighting me. I didn't know if he was surprised by my questions, but I desperately wanted to hear him say, "No."

He sounded more understanding, reassuring and compassionate than ever. He told me how he believed in me, and how he knew I could do it. But he thought it would be fun if we traveled together. I responded that if he was coming to protect me, then he shouldn't come. But if he really wanted to travel through Africa, he was welcome to join me.

In 2004, when I met Brian, I didn't think we would come this far. He was a reserved, but kind and generous man who socialized with only a few friends. He didn't say much, and that sort of suited me. There was so much going on in my life at the time, and all I had was more questions than answers.

On weekends, we'd go on long walks to the park, have long brunches where we'd both spend hours reading the Sunday paper without the need to talk except questions like, "Do you need more coffee?" He was conservative, and I am liberal, but that didn't bother us. We debated sometimes, with respect and understanding. We went on a date to secondhand book stores and had a picnic in winter in the car.

Brian showed up in my life after I ended an engagement with someone my parents had loved and respected and I hoped I would marry. My mother wasn't happy with me to say the least. I was feeling outcast and isolated from my family and friends, who were eager to get me married off.

Brian's ability to accept me for who I was, rather than what I did, or who I wanted to become, made me throw myself into the relationship. Brian didn't care about the clothes I wore or how my hair looked, and most of all, he didn't need any convincing to travel.

The simplicity of everything made me fall in love with him.

But the problem was, I wanted more.

Abyssinian Nomad

In 2005, after dating Brian for about a year, I had decided to go to Ethiopia to visit my family for a few months. Brian wanted to come with me, and we planned to visit South Africa and Kenya at the same time. It was his first trip to Africa, but I didn't think that would be a big deal. However, everything that could go wrong, went wrong in our time in Ethiopia. I was frustrated because the country had changed so much. I too felt like a tourist. We had to attend at least five of my Ethiopian friends' weddings, which meant a whole new experience, but not only that, everywhere we went people asked us, "So when are you getting married?" Brian, to his credit, tried to understand the culture and remain friendly toward people, but I could see it was a huge struggle for him. And though my family was trying to be warm and kind toward him, they hadn't forgiven me nor given up on the engagement I broke off. All that created so much pressure for both of us. Though I was very angry and frustrated, I also didn't want Brian to say anything bad or express his frustration about it; Ethiopia and Ethiopians became a very sensitive subject for us.

So when we came back to Montreal after three months, it was clear something had shifted and there was nothing that could fix it. But still we tried, without addressing any of it, until one day he said it wasn't working. I knew that too, but I wasn't brave enough to say it.

Now, a few years later, everything changed at lightning speed after I said "yes" to Brian. I had already sent out email requests to potential couchsurfing hosts, and now I would have to inform them that we were two. The question was, who was Brian? Brian, my ex-boyfriend? Brian, my friend? Or Brian, my potential boyfriend? Once again, I was uncertain. At that moment, there was nothing in my life that I was in control of. And it felt like the gods of uncertainty had taken over my life.

Brian shared my love for being on the road with the same intensity and desire. I could just imagine what it would mean for the two of us to travel through Africa. How could I say no to that trip?

Soon after I agreed he could travel with me, Brian started planning. He decided to buy a car online in Cape Town and return it later. Apparently, there were lots of travelers who bought cars in Cape Town and sold them in Egypt. But since he wasn't planning on going all the way to Cairo, he would drive back from Tanzania while I continued my journey north.

I wanted to cross Africa and meet and connect with people, hear stories, and experience life as it happens. Driving around would create distance from the very people I wanted to connect with. From experience, I knew that people wouldn't approach me if they thought I was different from them. But I didn't say no because I was still worried I needed to keep Brian safe, and if that meant driving then, yes, we would do it. I surrendered to the idea of driving, not wholeheartedly, but with understanding.

On December 31, 2007, a few hours before the New Year celebrations, Tascha and I (I was shaking) drove to O. R. Tambo Airport in Gauteng to welcome Brian, and we got home just in time for the New Year countdown. We welcomed it in with Canadian ice-wine, my favorite drink. I held the glass to wish both my best friend Tascha and Brian a happy New Year, and welcomed it with warmth, tingling, and hope in my heart.

There were no discussions or agreements, and before I knew it, I was back with Brian. I dived right back in where I had been, and where probably I didn't want to be, because it was so emotionally taxing for me. We spent the next few days exploring Johannesburg once again (we had been to Johannesburg together before), and spending time with my new friends I was lucky to be making in the couchsurfing community.

Brian was great at blending in. For most of my friends, they could finally put a face to the name they'd heard about so long. Seeing him with my new friends and knowing my mother's desire before she left South Africa, I gave in again. I felt the possibility of a happily-ever-after with Brian. It wasn't because things had changed for us. But, *"Who knows?"* I told myself.

At least I didn't feel guilty every time I talked to my mother and she asked about Brian. He was right there with me, and we were back together again.

Chapter 7: Walking the Labyrinth

*"It takes time to Flower, To Mature,
To come to the Centre of who we are
To find ourself and there Discover the Divine presence
in Truth and in Love"*
~ Unknown

I HAD REQUESTED A COUCH in Hogsback, Eastern Cape. The couple who offered us the couch seemed very welcoming and had promised the area was worth a visit. What we didn't know was it's believed Hogsback inspired J.R.R Tolkien's fictional Middle Earth.

But as we were nearing East London, I got an email from my sister, Selam, saying my mother had changed medicine and was getting weak. Also, she needed more painkillers, but had specifically warned Salem not to tell my other sister and me. My sister asked me to call my mother and talk to her without mentioning the new medication. *That didn't sound positive,* I thought.

I immediately called, and my mother sounded quite frail— she could hardly talk to me. Brian and I agreed that I should leave for Addis on the next available flight from the nearest town, which was Port Elizabeth. We'd need to drive to Port Elizabeth.

We decided to go for at least a day to meet the couchsurfers and see the Hogsback Mountains. The view as we were driving up the mountains was just breathtaking; I eagerly looked from side to side, trying not to miss any of the scenery It was lush green with a beautiful blue sky, and what awaited us on top was even more magical.

Unknown to us, our host actually owned a guesthouse, and had a room with a stunning view of the mountain already prepared for us. I thanked them and explained that we wouldn't be able to stay the night, but we were there to hang out for the rest of the day.

And that's when I saw the big labyrinth, its narrow, greenery-lined paths winding and circling inward to a beautiful stone center.

I couldn't believe we'd ended up standing in front of a labyrinth. The place was mystical and magical at the same time. The labyrinth was on a flat place near the top of the hill, overlooking broad forested ridges and valleys, with an expansive sky above me. Looking at the mountains and the enchanted forest, I felt the energy building within me. I breathed in and exhaled deeply, as if I hadn't breathed for days, feeling the lightness with each inhale and exhale. I took my shoes off and paused briefly in front of the entrance of the labyrinth with my heavy heart and wobbly legs, as if to say, *I am here. Tell me what I need to do?*

I remembered the three stages of the Christian tradition of walking a labyrinth, where the path from the entrance to the center represents shedding or "letting go." There is a release and an emptying of worries and concerns. At the center of the labyrinth you find illumination, insight, and focus. It is in the center that you are in a prayerful, meditative, receptive state.

Maskarm Haile

On the way out of the labyrinth, you integrate the insight you received, and are empowered to manifest it in the world.

Everything was an intense green that seemed to vibrate around the labyrinth, which instantly brought a sense of calm within me. I entered the labyrinth and made my way toward the center as slowly as possible, as if worried about disturbing its peace, but with a lot of urgency from within to convey my prayer for my mother.

In the past, I had walked a labyrinth in the hope of getting to know who I was, for my own spiritual growth, and with a sense of urgency to understand my calling. But this time, it was different, which made my last walk seem more like a luxury. I guess as humans, when we are faced with death, everything else becomes secondary. As I placed one foot forward after the other, I prayed for my mother, for her well-being and that she wouldn't suffer.

Tears rolling down my face, I said my quick serenity prayer under my breath.

"God grant me the serenity to accept the things I cannot change, courage to change the things I can, and wisdom to know the difference."

It was my first time trying to surrender to what was to come. At that point, I was attempting to keep it together, but inside, the thought of losing my mother was terrifying. But I kept reminding myself that it was neither the time nor the place for me to fall apart.

Once I got to the center, I sat on the ground for a little meditation, feeling much lighter in my head and body.

I gave my gratitude as I was walking back through the labyrinth, feeling hopeful and my wobbly legs were now steady. I felt a sense of peace within me beyond what I could ever have imagined. It was like the mountains were surrounding me and saying, "It's okay, Maski."

Chapter 8: Be Careful what You Wish For

"Can you think of any other place in the world where two Nobel Peace Prize winners lived on the same street? Both Nelson Mandela and Archbishop Desmond Tutu had houses on Vilakazi Street in Soweto."
~ Facts about South Africa

MY MOTHER WAS HAPPY TO see me even though she hadn't been expecting me. She was in bed, looking frail. I looked around for answers from my dad and sister. They all look tired. It seemed as if my sister read my mind and explained they had gone to see her doctor a few times already, and he confirmed the medication was too strong for her body. After I arrived, we went back to her doctor, who was a very renowned oncologist (the only one at that time in the country) and shuttled between the private and government hospital every day, seeing thousands of people. Earlier that morning, he had decided to get my mother admitted to the hospital. In Ethiopia, there is a lot of procedure for everything, and many papers to be signed and stamped by different people. It was late afternoon by the time we got her admitted, and the doctor was able to see her.

Maskarm Haile

While I was in the hospital with my mother in Ethiopia, I spoke to Brian at least once or twice a day. He was genuinely concerned about my mother, and he gave me the support I so desperately needed.

In the next few days my mother gained more energy: she was able to sit and eat food. I didn't leave the hospital except to take a shower, and eat. Hearing about my mother's admittance in the hospital, most of our relatives started to visit. Some of them I hadn't seen in over ten years. It was wonderful, to get reconnected and catch up on the news, yet no matter how I tried to make conversation, it always ended up being about me. Mostly the conversations started out like this:

"Weygood.... Keyet tegnish zaree?" (Where did you come from today?)

"Anchi beka alsemam alshe Aydel? Meen'ale leentishs sity tollo agbteshe lije betworldgi?" Which literally meant that if I decided to have child that very day, all my mother's sickness would miraculously disappear. That statement was then followed by:

"You know, you are running out of time to get married and have a child?" and "You might not even find a guy to marry you later!"

"Who's going to take care of you when you get old and sick if you don't have kids now?"

Of course, not wanting to hurt anyone's feeling or upset my mother, I didn't say anything, just tried to smile and shrugged my shoulders. But all I wanted to do was cry, and for my mom to come to my defense. But that didn't happen. So, I just tried to change the subject.

~~~

During my mother's second week in the hospital, the scene changed slowly. Having relatives and family friends come to visit my mom helped her to get better; it was also the first time in over fifteen years the entire family was in the same room.

Once again, we were full of hope. Two weeks after she got admitted to the hospital, the doctor suggested she could be discharged from in a few days if she continued to improve. That was good news; until then I had had no idea if I was going back to Cape Town as planned to continue my travels. So I flew to Cape Town feeling hopeful and very grateful my mother was feeling better. The worst had passed, I told myself, and nothing could go wrong if she continued with her medication.

I was happy to be back in Brian's arms, my safe haven after what I had just been through in Addis Ababa. At this point, I felt he was the only person who knew me well, understood how I lived, and allowed me to be me. And that freedom meant everything to me. He was also one of the few people who loved traveling as much as I did and was interested in the things that I do. I just wanted him to hold me and never let go.

What I went through in those short weeks had seemed like too much. It was a close call, almost losing my mother, and I was not ready for that, not then, and perhaps I never would be. I also felt that I'd been asked more annoying questions about my life than ever before. I was not the same person that I had been! Something had shifted within me, and I couldn't pinpoint it. I was mentally and physically exhausted.

Brian collected the car he had bought online and seemed to be pleased with the result. It looked to be in great condition and ready for the rough African roads ahead. For the first time, some part of me felt relieved. I was a little shaken from my interactions in Ethiopia, and I thought maybe the car would provide shelter at times. *Who knew?* Maybe this trip was going to be about defending my existence and desire to travel the world. I mean, if my family and friends didn't understand what I was doing, how would people from other African cultures understand me? For the first time, it actually seemed like a good idea to have a car.

~~~

Cape Town is one of the most picturesque, fascinating cities I've ever been to. It has wonderful weather, trendy cafes and restaurants, interesting bookstores, vibrant art galleries, and friendly people. Cape Town is also a great hub for travelers to embark on day trips to famous South African wineries along the Cape Wine Route: Robben Island, where Nelson Mandela was held prisoner for twenty-seven years, and Cape Agulhas, where the cold Atlantic Ocean and warm Indian Ocean meet.

Cape Town also has one of my favourite beaches—Boulder Beach, where I braved a swim in the cold Atlantic Ocean just because of the southern penguins. Of course, there is also the famous Table Mountain, which can be ascended either by taking a comfortable cable car or for the more adventurous, by hiking up it. Brian and I took our time to explore and enjoy once again the incredible natural beauty of Cape Town and its surroundings.

Before heading to the border of Namibia, we decided to stop at the Cape of Good Hope, the most southwestern point of the African continent. The stop at the Cape Point marked the official start of my Cape to Cairo journey. It was the last time I would absorb the breathtaking panoramic view of the mountains and ocean from the top of a mountain, and walk around the lighthouse. We took the famous cable train, "Flying Dutchman Funicular," leisurely taking in the natural beauty.

But even that gorgeous day didn't pass without a glitch. As we came down, we stopped at the souvenir shop to buy some cookies (my idea) to celebrate the official start of my Cape to Cairo journey. But the excitement was very short-lived. As the wind was getting strong, Brian, being the gentleman he always is, decided to bring the car closer so I wouldn't have to walk. I was left alone with the new bag of cookies I had just opened and my windbreaker I was trying to put on. Suddenly, I felt as if someone was looking at me. Unnerved, I slowly turned to look around. As I did so, my eyes locked with those of a full-grown male baboon. Terrified, I continued to look around and noticed that he was not alone: there were others starting to circle me. I tried to cover the cookies with my windbreaker, but before I knew it, the big baboon had darted toward me, knowing I had something in my hand. Suddenly, the cookies and my windbreaker dropped from my hand, and he was briefly distracted. Instead of coming for me, he ran to the cookies before his friends could get to them. As I stood relieved, trying to catch my breath, I noticed a tourist with a big camera taking my picture. He was obviously more intent on getting a good photo than he was in coming to my assistance. When did taking pictures become more important than saving someone's life, I wondered?

It was a beautiful, sunny, blue-sky day, and I was ready to leave South Africa. Our travels in South Africa had been enjoyable. For the most part, it was a place we revisited and reminisced about while we created new memories. We had met new people, visited some amazing places, and filled the car with everything we could imagine we might need for our long journey, including stocking our first-aid box.

We were both genuinely excited. The journey was starting to feel real. I said to myself that it would feel even more real when we crossed the first border, which wasn't too far away at that point. *This is it*, I thought, *there is no going back!*

I whispered my gratitude to the universe for everything, including the car, since it was allowing us to see places that would have been difficult to get to by hitchhiking. I was also incredibly grateful that the car afforded me the little alone time I needed after my Ethiopia trip.

The further north we drove, the more the vegetation changed. We entered the warm, dry region, a territory we had never before explored, and we had no idea what to expect. After driving for about two hours, our car suddenly stopped without warning. Luckily there was no traffic, and Brian managed to park the car at the side of the road. We didn't think there could be anything seriously wrong with it. We had entered the town of Springbok and thought the car had overheated because of the long drive. We used all the water we had in the car to cool it off and waited for a while, hoping it would start. It didn't.

Deep inside, I felt a little guilty, wondering if I had somehow jinxed the car and caused it to break down by not initially wanting it. We were in the middle of nowhere; we could see only a few farmhouses in the distance, and nothing else. We tried to call the company who sold the car to us, but there was no answer. It seemed that Friday afternoon wasn't a good time to have a breakdown at the side of the road. There was nothing much that could be done until Monday.

We managed to "push-drive" the car to one of the farmhouses. Our knock/honk was answered by a bright young Afrikaans boy who seemed shocked to see two strangers standing outside his gate. Not only that, but the strangers were a black-and-white couple, something he probably didn't see very often.

We introduced ourselves and explained how our car had stopped in the middle of the road. The curious young man, who must have been around fifteen years old, had no idea what we were saying, but he was quick to open the gate and to help push the car inside the compound where he lived. He later told us his name was Adonis. When his old grandfather came out and found us in the compound, he didn't share the same enthusiasm his young grandson had. He offered us water to drink—we had poured all our bottles of water on the car, hoping it would cool the vehicle and it would start.

The young man brought out his tools and started checking the car, looking very confident and seeming to know what he was doing. In the meantime, we called the AA (Automobile Association of South Africa) and asked them to send a tow truck to make sure we would be able to reach town before the garage closed for the weekend.

Our new friend, Adonis, almost banged his head on the hood of the car as he announced with one word, "Dead!" And then signaled to Brian, showing him that the engine was dead. Of course, we didn't believe him, or was it that some part of me felt he was right, but didn't want to accept it? Language was a barrier, but we showed Adonis a map of Canada where we came from and, using a map of Africa, showed him where we were heading. He was clearly sad for us, confirming and reconfirming there was no way the car was getting us anywhere.

When the tow truck finally arrived, the driver assured us we would get to the only garage in town before it closed. It was indeed a weird feeling to see the car on the back of the tow truck. At the garage, the mechanic confirmed the young man's diagnosis: the engine was dead and there was nothing that could be done. He would need a few days to take out the engine and see what could be done to repair it.

All we could do was find a place to stay and hire a rental car for a few days while he figured out our car's fate.

We spent the next few days exploring that beautiful place that we would have otherwise just passed by without getting a chance to discover. We made Port Nolloth our base as we toured the Alexander Bay area. For over 150 years, it has been an occasionally rowdy seaport catering to copper miners, seafarers, diamond divers, fishermen and, nowadays, overland travelers with a sense of adventure. We also tried to catch up on our reading, and we cooked at the hotel apartment facing the beautiful ocean where we stayed, trying to make our stay as relaxed as possible. The town was tiny, and nothing much happened, but the ocean was beautiful.

The mechanic confirmed the engine had seized. Brian called the sellers to let them know, but they refused to believe that the engine was the problem. We finally managed to get them to take the car back, and they sent a tow truck to collect the car, while we decided to travel Africa as I had originally planned.

Something within me danced again! But this time, it was a kind of victory dance. After Brian had made the plans and arrangement with the car, I hadn't anticipated being able to travel Africa as I had originally intended. The past few days, I had been wondering if my desire not to travel in the car that manifested in all the problems with it. Of course, I didn't share these thoughts with Brian. He would probably have dismissed it by saying I was crazy. But in any case, now we needed a plan, a good plan. The car had been packed with our camping equipment, books, food and supplies—everything we thought would make our camping and travels as comfortable as possible. Getting a new car was out of the question because getting permits to cross the border of each country by car takes a long time. We were in luck: there was a car rental company in Springbok that would allow us to return the rental in Windhoek, the capital of Namibia. It was the only reasonable plan we could come up with at the time. We finally filled our small rental car trunk and back seat and headed to the border.

Chapter 9: God Must Be Crazy

"The Namib desert, at 80 million years, is the world's oldest desert. Namib means 'open space.'"
~ 22 fun facts about Namibia

AT LAST, WE SAW THE border signpost. It read, "Welcome to The Republic of Namibia." The red, tanned soil and crossing the Orange River confirmed we had entered a new territory. The border crossing was free, quick, and uneventful. We showed our passports, yellow fever cards, and rental car permit and we were given a ninety-day tourist visa.

Brian and I were both in a good mood and impressed by the efficiency and friendliness of the border agents. The good infrastructure that reaches to just about every popular tourist destination in that country showed why Namibia is considered a great place for travelers to Africa.

I wanted to visit most of the countries on my itinerary because of the people I had met, books I had read, or movies I had watched. Watching *The Gods Must Be Crazy* in the 80s, set in the Kalahari Desert, had created the image of vastness, and vivid colors and space in my mind. I wondered and dreamt about that burnt sand-looking place for years. I just couldn't believe it when I was finally there.

Our first stop was "The Fish River Canyon," and we headed to the campground early enough to set up our tents and watch the sunset. It felt good to be with other travelers, to swap stories and share tips. As we sat sipping South African wine and watching the beautiful red sunset, we started talking to random travelers. Though there were lots of campers, most traveling only around Namibia. One of the most inspiring travelers we met that night was a German who was biking solo from Cairo to Cape Town. It was amazing to meet someone who was on the same kind of journey as me. The fact that he was only one border away from finishing his epic travel adventure made me think that what I was doing was truly possible. It was a great confirmation to meet someone who was actually in the journey, rather than just reading a book about others' experiences.

The next morning, we woke early, excited about our day. The Fish River Canyon is the biggest in Africa and the second largest in the world. I was in awe and high from just being there. The Fish River is the longest river in Namibia, with a length of 650 km. It is famous for its long hike of 86 km, which takes about five to six days. We settled for a day visit. I was struck by the massive beauty of the canyon from the moment I stood overlooking it. We walked around most of the day taking in the spectacular formation, amazingly sculpted cliffs, and the color of the canyon from different viewpoints, occasionally graced by beautiful bird life.

I was feeling bummed about not being able to hike the canyon because of my knee problem. Years of track running and hiking had taken a toll on both my knees, which led to endless anti-inflammatory medication, surgery, and years of physiotherapy.

We decided to camp for the night at Ai-Ais natural hot spring and soothe our bodies. Ai-Ais means "burning water." The spring is a sulphur-rich hot spring full of minerals. According to Lonely Planet, it sounded like a very busy and popular place, but when we arrived, there was hardly anyone around. We had to find the employee in order to pay to go inside the spa.

The fact we were the only customers didn't bother me. I liked the tranquil environment. The spa employee came inside to show us the male and female changing rooms and showers. I told Brian I'd meet him by the indoor pool and went to change my clothes.

When I came out, Brian was nowhere to be seen. I went straight to the pool but when he didn't show up for few minutes, I decided to check on him and headed to the male changing room. Brian was standing outside the changing room and when our eyes met, he put his hands on his mouth to say, *be quiet.* And with his hand again he showed me the big cobra that was standing between us.

The only thing Brian had in his hand were his swimming shorts he was about to change into, and I was standing in my bikini, nothing else. As we both stood there, not knowing what would happen, the cobra darted away and we lost sight of him. When we finally found the courage to move and call the employees, a couple of them came with sticks to look for the cobra, assuring us we were safe by the pool. I was already in my bikini; there was no turning back.

"Reptiles and insects are in abundance. You may encounter huge iguana lizards, Cape cobras, black spitting cobras, puff adders and horned adders. Different species of locusts, butterflies, and moths are also present." *(One of the signs at Fish River Canyon Camping Ground)*

I was beginning to realize they weren't kidding with the sign! We had already seen a few of the things mentioned, and for someone like me, who's only fear is anything that crawls, camping was becoming less and less appealing by the day.

After almost a week's delay, we reached the house of our couchsurfing host, Ajit, in Windhoek. He didn't mind that we were late, and he turned out to be one of the most gracious, fun, and generous couchsurfing hosts we were lucky to stay with. He opened his heart and home for us. He was witty, curious, and open. Originally from India, he had been living in Namibia for most of his life. He loved the country, and it was refreshing and fun to be around him. He lived, alone, in a big house, and we were given one of his grown kids' rooms. Given our circumstance with the car, he said that we were welcome to stay as long as we needed to in order to sort our plans.

When we woke up the next morning, we found another couchsurfer had arrived in the early morning, and that Ajit had gone to pick her up. She was a young Mongolian who had come from North Africa, the exact opposite route to what I wanted to do, but the second traveler I had met who was doing the same trip I was. It is incredible how we easily connect with people who share the same goals and dreams. She was the first Mongolian couchsurfer I had met, but not only that, she was one border away from completing her trip, just like the German biker we had met at the campground in Fish River Canyon. Finding a brave, solo, female traveler inspired me even more. I instantly liked her. Ajit sat with us and circled on a big Namibian map all the places we shouldn't miss visiting. He also got us a discount on a stay at the Etosha National Park, and we offered a ride to our new Mongolian friend. I found her to be inspiring and full of anecdotes about her wonderful travels. More than anything, I found her goal intriguing: 100 countries before she turned thirty, and then get married a couple months later. All I could wish for was that my family and friends would meet this woman.

Connecting with Ajit was easy. He was a very charismatic, free-spirited, and passionate person who loved the country he lived and knew it well. He always had his map ready to help travelers experience the best of Namibia. He offered to make us a proper Indian meal, which meant we had to go out grocery shopping. We came back with a few bags of fresh vegetables, chicken, and herbs. After being on the road for few weeks and mostly eating fast camping food or at restaurants, the idea of eating a homemade meal was mouth-watering. But then we also discovered that Ajit was a fantastic cook. The feast included my favorite Indian dessert, homemade Gulab Jamun. I was in heaven.

In the middle of one of our conversations, Ajit and I discovered we had gone to the same college, Madras Christian College (MCC), in South India. It was like finding a long-lost old friend all over again. We weren't in the same year, but the fact that we had both walked on the same campus bonded us even more. MCC is a unique place, and no matter which year we were there, it will always be an amazing experience to meet a fellow "MCCian" around the world.

Before I had even finished my thought about how grateful I was and how things were falling into place, Ajit suggested we should watch *The Gods Must Be Crazy* on his projector. How was that for a coincidence?

Our next destination was the Sossusvlei sand dunes. For the last few days, my heart had been beating quicker just at the thought of it. It's one of Namibia's highlights, and I had fallen in love with the color of the sand ever since I had seen amazing pictures and numerous documentaries on the Discovery Channel. Our adventure started when we went to pick up the car we'd rented online, and it wasn't available. The car rental company decided to give us a bigger 4X4 pickup. We weren't very thrilled about that, but we took the vehicle and drove to Sesriem at night to set up camp so we could wake up early and drive to see the sunrise.

Maskarm Haile

Looking at the road, we quickly realized we were lucky to have the 4X4. It would have been difficult to navigate a small car on that road. By the time we reached the park, all our bags, camping gear, and everything we had put in the back was covered with fine red sand, and the truck had a flat tire.

As soon as it got dark, the seemingly endless night sky filled with stars once again, making us forget our tiredness, the challenges we had faced on the bad road, and the red sand. We sat there in silence, holding each other's hands and covering ourselves to keep warm in the chilly desert night.

As I went to bed and looked at the stars from our small tent window, I prayed for my mom's well-being. I was so happy to be in Namibia and couldn't believe my good fortune. A sense of gratitude warmed my heart, and I knew that when I woke up in the morning, I would be walking on those ancient red sand dunes that I had seen on TV years ago.

Namibia blew my mind: looking at the place where the desert meets the ocean, the wildlife in Etosha, close encounters with thousands of Cape Cross seals, the picturesque Salt Lake, watching the sunrise in Sossusvlei desert and the sunset in Swakopmund, and climbing sand dunes. The moment of truth took place when we got back to Ajit's home for one last time after exploring beautiful Namibia. We couldn't carry all our stuff. So, Ajit once again rescued us and bought all our camping gear from us. But not only that, knowing we still had the rental car with us, he said he had a plan. We had no idea what he was going to say. He had done a lot for us already, and we weren't expecting anything from him. He said his plan was simple...

We would all wake up at two in the morning, pack our stuff in the rental car, and drive to the Botswana border while he slept in the back of the car. He would then drive back, drop the car at the car rental company, and go to work in the morning. His help was nothing but a form of divine intervention.

Abyssinian Nomad

Often, I called my mother to share some of my stories, and I frequently omitted things like the car breaking down in the middle of nowhere, and driving to the border at two in the morning. She sounded well, and the calls seemed to lift her spirits.

Chapter 10: Under the Clear African Sky

"The Okavango Delta is the largest inland delta in the world, covering an area of 15,000 km2 during drier times. During wetter periods, it can reach a staggering size of 22,000 km2."
~ 50 interesting facts about Botswana

IT WAS STILL DARK, AROUND five in the morning, when we reached the Botswana border. After we said our goodbyes to our new friend Ajit, we found a corner to sit and wait for the border to open. It was also too early to go around asking for a ride. There were lots of trucks waiting. Most people were waiting in their cars, some still sleeping.

It was another easy border crossing, but finding transportation that was going north was not so simple. A lot of the people were going to Gaborone, the capital of Botswana. After crossing the border, we walked to the gas station, where we managed to talk to a truck driver who was willing to drop us at an intersection where we might stand a better chance of getting a ride to Manu, the gateway to the Okavango Delta.

Abyssinian Nomad

A few minutes after crossing the Botswana border, we climbed aboard a huge truck with a friendly driver who made space for our stuff (we were down to two backpacks and two full daypacks). It was my first time inside a truck like that. I was pleasantly surprised with the comfortable sleeping space it had. But sleep was far from my mind. Rain had started to pour outside. I love the rain, and I love the smell of the wet soil in the country. As a child, when I was growing up in Ethiopia, I loved the sound of the raindrops hitting the bedroom roof while I slept. Though I loved playing in the rain, our families didn't allow children to play in the rain, saying they would catch cold.

Even with the heavy rain and mist, I could still see there wasn't much traffic on the road. Brian was talking to our new friend, explaining our relationship, and where we met, and what we were doing in Africa to yet another surprised person who didn't seem to understand. I wondered how we were going to get a ride if there was no traffic on the road; how long would it take us to get a lift?

Nature was in abundance and everything seemed intensely green, but it was also clear that apart from the bush, there was nothing around. We were in the middle of nowhere. I was mesmerized and thrilled to be able to travel as I had wanted and imagined it for years. There was a sense of freedom and vulnerability that came with it. Then suddenly it dawned on me: what if something happened to Brian? To us? Thinking about all the warnings I had received from family and friends, I had a moment of panic. I quickly looked at Brian. He and the driver were engaged in a deep conversation. I felt relieved because Brian was also making the journey for his own reasons. I couldn't take responsibility for everything. I also couldn't worry that something might happen to one or both of us, when all we'd experienced so far were gifts of human generosity in every form.

Maskarm Haile

The rain let up, and we got dropped off at the next intersection. There was absolutely nothing around it except a signpost for drivers. We jumped out of the truck with our backpacks, thanked the driver and said goodbye once again. We found ourselves standing on the roadside.

I had imagined that moment for months, and as much as the thought had scared me to death, it never once made me change my plan. I asked Brian if he was okay and if he thought the journey was worth it. He said "yes" to both. I was happy we were still on the same page, and I felt encouraged.

It was still drizzling; we put our backpacks on the wet ground and sat on them by the side of the road. No traffic was heading in the direction we wanted to go, but a few cars passed by in the other direction. We were talking and laughing about our experiences and joking that we might have to walk for miles to find humans. But after about thirty minutes, which felt much longer, a car zoomed past us and then suddenly stopped at the intersection. We thought it had stopped for us, so with our backpacks in hand, we ran to the car.

The driver, a young black South African man, hadn't even seen us sitting on the side of the road, or if he had, he didn't realize that we were hitchhiking. He just couldn't hide his amusement that anyone in their right mind would start out on such a journey without a plan—or a car. He said he'd been driving the whole night and was in a hurry to get to Kasane for a business meeting. Brian and I looked at each other, hoping we would be able to get a lift. He explained he had stopped his car at the intersection to drop off a local person he had given a lift. We asked if he could give us a ride, explaining where we wanted to go. He didn't seem sure.

We said it would be perfect if he could drop us in Maun.

"Maun?" he said, puzzled.

Then we understood: he must be lost. The local person had guided him to where we were and had left. The driver had no idea how he was to get to Kasane. It was our turn to be surprised. He didn't have a map or GPS.

Brian took out our map in the rain, showed him where Kasane was and explained he needed to drive through Maun.

Looking relieved, the driver quickly gave his car key to Brian, opened the back door of his car, climbed in and went to sleep.

We couldn't believe our luck! The truth is, we still don't even know his name.

Brian drove through the rain and fog, breathing in the fresh earthy air and taking in the beautiful view that went far and beyond our imagination. The tarmac road was almost empty of traffic, but both sides were surrounded by green forest.

When we arrived in Maun, our friend woke up feeling refreshed and ready to tackle the rest of the way. There wasn't much time to chat or get to know each other. I gave him a quick hug to say thank you and good luck, the guys exchanged handshakes, and he drove away.

We stayed about ten kilometers outside of Maun, in what is considered the gateway to the Okavango. The Old Bridge Backpackers Hostel offered a package that allowed travelers to use it as a base to explore the delta. We took the package and opted for a three-day, fully catered canoeing trip to the heart of the delta in a "mokoro," a traditional dug-out canoe.

I don't remember meeting people from Botswana when I was growing up, but what I do know about Botswana was planted in my mind a long time ago from a documentary on the Okavango Delta. I remember thinking the elephants looked majestic and the land seemed wild. For years, I was obsessed with the wildlife in the Okavango Delta. Though I had already been on safaris in different parts of Africa, my obsession remained.

Maskarm Haile

Unfortunately, the very first wild animal I saw was a zebra chewing a plastic bag at the side of the road, and the sight of that just broke my heart.

We woke up early the next morning to get ready to be picked up at 7:30 a.m. We needed to pack light, mostly rain gear and walking shoes—things we could fit in the small mokoro boat. Mokoro boats are long, narrow canoes traditionally made from dug-out tree trunks and have been used by locals for fishing and transporting goods for hundreds of years. And, these days, they are the most popular transport for tourists in the Delta. We got into a 4X4 vehicle and drove the dirt road for about two hours before we were dropped off at the mokoro station, where we were introduced to a small-featured man with a big smile who was going to be our river guide and cook for the next three days. I was beyond excited!

The gentle guide explained how he would find a nice campsite for us since there was no designated camping place in the Delta, which made it both fun and challenging in the rainy season. Nevertheless, he promised the experience over the following three days would be unforgettable. Looking at our surroundings, far from everything we knew, I sort of trusted him.

For starters, getting on the small mokoro was as terrifying as it was exciting. Brian was a very tall man, and I wasn't sure how his legs were going to fit. Sitting in the boat was a balancing act, and being on that small boat in the Delta was a surreal moment. "Oh my God!" I said to myself. I wanted to pinch myself, and jump up and down, as if to wake up from the dream I felt I was in. I looked up at the clear blue sky … just to whisper once again my gratitude.

For a place filled with so much life, it was surprisingly quiet. In fact, the air and the stillness not only affected my breathing, but calmed my entire body and mind, one breath at a time. The peacefulness of the place, accompanied by the birds singing and the wind blowing on my face, created overwhelming joy from within that I hadn't felt in a long time. The vibrant nature around me resonated within me, and I felt at one with it.

After navigating the Delta for a while, our guide spotted a place he felt would make a good campsite. We helped pitch our tent and gathered wood for the fire, knowing it would be a challenge to start a fire with wet wood. The rain had come back in full force once again, making the entire forest seem enchanted with the buzzing of the insects and the croaking of the frogs. The ground had a rich, earthy smell. It seemed as if all my senses had come alive.

The instruction from the guide was simple, but firm: "You do not leave this area without me, under any circumstances!" The reason was apparent. There was no fancy electronic fence to keep the animals (hippos, elephants, lions) away from the humans. Everything was done in the daylight, and after an early dinner by the fireside, we called it a day.

Back in Maun, the person we'd talked to at the Backpackers' Hostel had passionately spoken about how unique the experience of the walking safari would be for us. But I had two issues with that. One was my knee problem; I had no idea if I could walk for five hours, but that was a minor problem that could easily be fixed with some painkillers. The second and more important issue was my fear. I had heard stories in South Africa of people getting out of their car in the national parks and being eaten by lions. And the walking safari would be in lion and other wildlife territories!

Though our guide was a small man, he was full of confidence. He stated he was a very famous hunter in his tribe and promised nothing would happen to us. Not feeling reassured and because I didn't see any weapon on him, I asked how he planned to protect us. He quickly pointed to a small knife that was tied to one of his legs. I just looked at Brian.

Maskarm Haile

Our guide walked ahead of us, occasionally stopping to explain what sort of wildlife we might encounter. Picking up bones and stones, he educated us on how to track wildlife and helped us understand the movement, patterns, and behavior of different animals. After walking through the bush for some time, we arrived at an open plain where we stood in the center and were watched by the wild animals from afar. The sun was getting hotter, and we were worried that the animals would soon look for shade under the trees. Our guide was quick to reassure us that we would not be resting in the shade for too long, and soon we carried on with our walk.

I can certainly say that the bushwalks I had been on before paled into insignificance when compared with that walking safari. Our guide gave us more details, and we saw fresh animal paw prints, smelt fresh elephant dung, and saw the bones of dead animals, while we watched the giraffes and a family of elephants from afar and we walked among impalas, kudus, wildebeest, zebras and waterbucks.

Our three-day experience in the Okavango Delta was exceptional. It cleared up a lot of space in my mind and heart; it thrilled me. I had never experienced the feeling of being so free, without shelter to run to or a car to use for hiding, nor any weapon to give a sense of security (even if it's false security). We were in a vast, wild, peaceful veldt that seemed endless. We were open and vulnerable in a way that is hard to describe. Perhaps the best thing I can compare it to is the rush of free-falling as you skydive. But this time, the breathtaking grandeur and sense of adventure came from my body and soul connecting with the beautiful land and water of the Okavango Delta.

Chapter 11: The Smoke that Thunders

"The noise of Victoria Falls can be heard from an almighty distance of 40 kilometers, while the spray from the falling water rises to 400 meters and reaches a distance of 50 kilometers. The nearby forest is incredibly luscious as it receives 'rain' from the falls 24 hours a day."
~ Seven Facts You Didn't Know About Zambia, from fastjet blog

IT WAS OUR SECOND BORDER crossing by foot. Getting the exit visa in the northern part of Botswana was easy—all we had to do was to walk to the river, where we crossed on a small ferry and presented our tourist visas and yellow fever cards. It seemed like the peaceful and free border crossings were almost over, since the road was getting bad and there would be no more free visas for Canadians. From now on, most of the countries we'd be passing through would require us to have visas in advance, or if not, to pay on arrival at the border crossing.

When we got off the ferry and started walking to the border post, touts for taxis and currency exchange followed us. They seemed a little aggressive, knowing that most tourists crossing at that border were going to Victoria Falls.

Maskarm Haile

Our first stop in Zambia was Livingstone, the southern province of Zambia named after the Scottish missionary and explorer David Livingstone. For me, Zambia was all about Victoria Falls. For most of my life, I had dreamed of seeing the falls, ever since I learned about it in my geography class in junior school. My mother had pictures from both the Zimbabwean and Zambian sides of the bridge. As a child, those pictures had intrigued me and piqued my interest.

When we got near the falls, my excitement peaked and I couldn't wait another minute to visit it. We dropped our bags at the Livingstone Backpackers' Hostel where we were staying and immediately set off to explore the magnificent Victoria Falls. No photo or video could ever have prepared me for what I saw, heard, and felt standing at the edge of the falls. We quickly realized the ponchos we'd bought to protect us from the spray of the falls were ineffective. In a matter of minutes, we were soaking wet.

It was hard to get a direct look at the falls because the rainy season had increased the amount of water gushing down and caused the powerful spray to foam like a white cloud over us. Added to that enchanted cloud-like, sopping wet experience, was the roar of the water falling and landing in the Zambezi River below it. The great thundering drowned out any other noise and captivated me. I can truly say that at that particular moment, I was living in the present and experienced a sense of being that was unlike anything I have felt in my life.

"...*creeping with awe to the verge, I peered down into a large rent... and saw that a stream of a thousand yards broad leaped down a hundred feet, and then became suddenly compressed into a space of fifteen or twenty yards... the most wonderful sight I had witnessed in Africa.*" [2]

"*No one can imagine the beauty of the view from anything witnessed in England. It had never been seen before by European eyes; but scenes so lovely must have been gazed upon by angels in their flight.*" [3]

---

[2] https://en.wikisource.org/wiki/Author_talk:David_Livingstone
[3] http://knowledgenuts.com/2013/11/28/africa-is-a-roman-name

The locals' name for Victoria Falls was Mosi-Oa-Tunya, which means "The Smoke that Thunders."

The bus station in Livingston looked organized, with clean buses to Lusaka. But I was surprised to see the number of preachers dressed in suits preaching on the buses. We had listened to lots of old country music on public transport and were mostly quoted Biblical texts when we were inside private cars and trucks, but it was my first time to see such well-dressed preachers. They didn't care whether we were Christian, Muslim, Hindu or even non-believers; they got on the busses with their Bibles to preach as if we were in church on Sunday morning.

When the preacher on our bus didn't get off as it started to move, I worried he would continue traveling with us and preach all the way to Lusaka. As the bus got moving, he asked us to pray with him for our safe journey and then spoke out against witchcraft before quickly jumping off the bus. No one seemed concerned or bothered by him. It was, I guess, business as usual for most people.

After the excitement of the preacher, Brian and I became the center of attention. People started to look and whisper to each other as if they were trying to figure out something. I saw them look at me, then Brian, and then back to me again.

I was looking forward to meeting people and had thought the bus would be a perfect opportunity, but unfortunately, making local friends turned out to be hard. Except for the touts at the border posts, it felt like most people would not approach a woman traveling with a man. I thought a possible reason for such behavior was a patriarchal system of respect between men. But then, I heard Brian starting a conversation with a young man who was sitting in our row. I tried to join in the conversation and even introduced my name, but to no avail. The man didn't acknowledge my presence apart from the occasional glance. He started to ask Brian questions about me.

Maskarm Haile

> Him: "Where is she from?"
> Brian: "Montreal."
> Him: "Montreal?"
> Brian: "Yes. Montreal, Canada."
> Him: "Ah..." (Looking a little confused.)
> Him: "She looks African."
> Brian: "Yes, she's originally from Ethiopia."

Before I knew it, I felt sad and frustrated. I was on my journey because I wanted to meet people, learn about the African continent, and share something, even if it meant sharing only a moment, some laughs and stories. I had noticed how people looked at us sometimes with curiosity and sometimes with confusion. Some asked if Brian had met me on his travels and kind of brought me along. He tried to make light of their comments, saying, "If they only knew." But for some reason, I felt hurt and a little frustrated. They didn't seem to acknowledge me as an African woman who was making the journey in her own right. It seemed that in their minds, my white boyfriend was the decision-maker, the one with money and with power, and I was just an "insignificant other." I wondered if people would treat me differently if I were traveling alone. Would they be as curious about me as I was about them if I were on the bus by myself? Would they still be suspicious of my intention, or would they give me the benefit of the doubt as a traveler?

We didn't have much planned for Lusaka except meeting up with Bupe, a local couchsurfer, for drinks—which later became dinner. Bupe was not only friendly but also an exceptionally funny, articulate, and informed young man. He explained to us the devastating effect of **HIV/AIDS** that left lots of youth dead and orphaned children to be raised by the elderly in Zambia.

At the time of our journey, HIV/AIDS was still the deadliest epidemic in the 21st century in Africa. The news was the same in the East African countries too. Hearing Bupe's personal journey with losing friends and people he knew very closely touched my heart, and I was grateful for his openness to share and his deep understanding of the situation.

My experience in Zambia felt like more of a transit rather than a deep travel experience. There was no getting lost in the local market, meeting strangers in a village or even aimlessly wandering around the city and talking to strangers. I kept thinking how it would have been wonderful if I'd had a chance to meet more young people like Bupe and engage in deep and meaningful conversation. I left Zambia feeling there is more to the country and to the people that I needed to explore someday. Victoria Falls was an undeniably magical experience, but I know for sure there must be more magic in Zambia than I have found so far.

Chapter 12: The Poor Billionaire

"The Zimbabwean dollar was introduced in 1980. The exchange rate at the time was $Z1 = US$1.47, but in 2008, Zimbabwe experienced a whopping 231 million percent inflation."
~ Wikipedia

AFTER HAGGLING OVER THE PRICE of bus tickets, we finally made it to Kariba, the border crossing into Zimbabwe. Feeling excited but a little apprehensive, we each approached the friendly immigration officers at a different window. One of the immigration officers was quick to recognize my features as Ethiopian, and a couple more agents started to gather around and ask me questions.

Brian was at another window getting his visa done, so the officers had no idea I was traveling with anyone. They didn't ask, and I didn't volunteer. But it was evident they didn't believe I was a traveler. When I finally produced my Canadian passport, some of them debated whether they should give me a discount on my visa. Of course, that wasn't going to work, but I thought the way they switched from being suspicious to wanting to give me a discount was funny!

I wanted to go to Zimbabwe because I had heard so much about how developed it was and how beautiful a country it was. But unfortunately for Zimbabwe, it was the worst time, a couple of months before the elections. The news coming out of Harare wasn't very encouraging, and we weren't sure that we should go at all. The media showed images of empty supermarkets and the long queues of people waiting to buy bread. There was even a warning about traveling to Zimbabwe on a travel advice website site.

I had received only one couchsurfing reply from a couchsurfing host in Harare. Marco accepted my request but also warned me about the situation in Zimbabwe. It was just before the general elections, and tensions in the country were running high. He couldn't assure us that we would be entirely safe if we wanted to travel outside Harare. He also advised that although fruits and greens were in abundance at the time, we should make sure we came fully equipped with basic supplies like soap, toothpaste, lotions, etc.

I sent out another email, thanking him for agreeing to host us and asking him and his family if they wanted anything from Lusaka. His reply was a simple, "Nutella + Nutella + Nutella, and a bottle of red wine!" Judging by his response, I knew I would get along very well with Marco and his family, being chocoholics like me.

My first lesson in Zimbabwe was that whatever you do, do not use your credit card. After years of international isolation, hyperinflation in Zimbabwe hit a record of 500 billion percent in 2008.

Though exchanging money on the black market was illegal and not easy to find, the difference in the exchange rates was huge. When we managed to change our US dollars on the black market, we suddenly became billionaires. We got a stack of Zim Dollar 10,000,000 notes in a bag. At the time, Zim Dollar 10,000,000 was equal to US $4, and that hardly bought breakfast. For the next few days, we walked around town with cash in a plastic bag to pay for our coffee, entrance to the park, lunch, and dinner. Sometimes we left a few bags in Marco's car to avoid carrying bags filled with cash. For the most part, the waiters or the owners of the cafes or restaurants didn't bother to count the money.

Unfortunately, because of tensions due to the upcoming elections, we weren't able to travel outside Harare. After spending a few days with Marco and his family wandering around the city, the highlight of my visit was when Marco drove us to the lion and cheetah park which is located about thirty minutes outside Harare. This popular sanctuary is a lion enclosure that allow visitors to get very close to the majestic animals, and the bravest guests pet and play with the young lions for a little extra fee to support the animal sanctuary. The star of the park is Tommy, believed to be a 300-year-old Galapagos tortoise, weighing in at around 500 kg. He seemed to be everyone's favorite. Marco told us anecdotes about how his grandparents use to bring him to the park when he was a child. Today he brings his child to the park. Tommy the tortoise has his own house he goes into every day at around four p.m., always taking the same route.

We were ready to leave Zimbabwe. But how? Somehow we were lucky getting a bus to Harare on the way in, but because of the lack of gas and the low number of people traveling, there was no regular bus that went to the border. So Marco dropped us off at an intersection where he thought we might be able to hitch a ride. We stood, in the full sun, at the side of a dusty road, for what felt like an eternity before a pickup first passed us and then reversed back. Rolling his window down and half climbing out of it, a young white man asked if we were lost. He seemed young, but his face looked tired and wrinkled, and his voice sounded rough.

Abyssinian Nomad

We explained we needed to get to the border, which was about 280 km from where we were. He wasn't sure if he had heard us right at first, but then got out of his car, introduced himself as Mike, and he said that we might be there for a long while.

We almost agreed with him. We had been there for more than thirty minutes and his was the first car we saw.

After thinking and examining us, appearing a little confused, Mike said he lived on a farm close to Marondera, and he was willing to take us to that town at least. With the bad road, he added, it might be about two hours. He didn't seem comfortable leaving us on the road.

We thanked him for the offer and jumped onto his pickup. I told Brian to sit in front, and I took a seat in the back. Knowing the issues in the country and Mike being a white farmer in Zimbabwe, I couldn't help but wonder how he felt giving a black girl a ride. Or did I get this ride because Brian was with me, and according to lots of people in South Africa and Zimbabwe, he can pass as white South African?

When I turned back into the conversation, Mike was saying, with resignation and a hint of sadness in his voice, that he hoped we were able to see something and enjoy his beautiful county.

The truth was, we didn't see much in Zimbabwe. We told him how we played with lion cubs and hung around in Harare, not being able to leave town for security reasons. I also told him I tried to see/meet Mengistu Haile Mariam, the ex-Ethiopian president, who has been living in Harare since he fled Ethiopian in 1991. We all laughed, thinking that was silly to even try to see him. He's highly protected by the president of Zimbabwe.

Then Brian asked Mike, "Were you born here?"

Mike: "Born and raised on the farm. I'm third-generation white African."

Maskarm Haile

Brian: "Do you still feel African after what is happening to farmers in Zimbabwe?"

Mike: (turning to look at Brian and looking at me in his front mirror) "Zimbabwe is a beautiful country, though some of the horror stories you hear are true. My family's land is full of squatters right now, and we also have some family who were kicked off their farms. But the community in Zimbabwe is very tight—blacks and whites help each other and want peace in the country."

Mike sounded more hopeful than anyone I have met, black or white, and the way he talked about Zimbabwe's future touched my heart. How did he find the faith and courage to believe, in the middle of the crisis?

We offered to give money for gas, but he refused to accept it, so we thanked him and jumped off his pickup. He looked at us once again in his rearview mirror and he sped away.

I put my backpack down to sit on it and started reading the big Africa Lonely Planet guidebook I was carrying. For the first time, it felt like we were actually on a lonely planet: though we were on the main road, there was hardly a car passing. It was quite hot, dusty, and our water tested like lukewarm tea.

There was no plan B except, if it got late, we would have to walk to the closest village and ask if we could spend the night. But then as we were entertaining that thought, an old silver Toyota passed us. Brian and I both jumped and signaled for the driver. It looked like a family with two kids in the back. Looking at the car almost full with people and stuff, we almost gave up, but we saw the car stop and slowly reverse toward us.

The man came out of the car and explained he and his family were going to Mutare. Mutare is just 10 km away from the border, and we almost jumped with excitement, but the question was where we were going to sit. The car was full and we also had our backpacks. The man just smiled and said, "No problem. We do this the African way." He opened the trunk and moved around his boxes and stuff and pushed our backpacks in, also moving some of the things from the back seat to the trunk. When the trunk wasn't closing, he took out a rope and tied the trunk door so it wouldn't flap and nothing would fall.

Inside the car, he asked his older daughter to hold her brother, which we protested, and we all found a way to share the seat.

The Zimbabwean family was going to Mutare to visit a family member. They said whatever they had in the car was to give to them—anything to help the family at this time. They told us despite its worthlessness, the Zimbabwean dollar was a scarce commodity. Banks rationed them—you could only withdraw a limited amount, which meant queueing every day for an ATM, gas, and bread, which took between four to six hours and sometimes more. They said it was the worst time they had ever experienced. They didn't sound angry or bitter about the situation, but just sad. When we asked about the upcoming election, and if they were going to vote, they both said it was pointless. They'd just give everything to God.

We shared some trail mix with the family and gave candies to the kids. For sure it was a luxury item for them at that moment. The old car was steaming, hardly able to move most of the way, but we still made it to Mutare. The kind man offered to drop us at the border since it wasn't going to be easy finding other transportation, and we insisted on giving him money for the gas.

Chapter 13: Lost in Translation

"Involvement in spiritualistic practices and belief in spiritualism are very rife in Mozambique. For example, every death in Mozambique is connected with witchcraft of evil spirit. [sic] And men are not allowed to drop a tear when someone dies. Men weeping when a death occurs is like a taboo."
~ *10 interesting facts about Mozambique*

LEAVING ZIMBABWE SAFELY WAS A huge accomplishment, especially successfully hitchhiking all the way to the border. But one thing was clear: we no longer had the luxury of good roads, and efficient and organized border agents. As much I wanted to celebrate the border crossing and enjoy the change of landscape, having to deal with aggressive touts and bargaining for transportation was a nightmare.

It had been a long day for both of us. We were tired, hungry, and eager to find a shower or at least a bucket of water to wash away the dust and the sticky sweat from our bodies. I was already irritated to say the least when the touts started to grab my backpack, some grabbing my hand and saying, "Sister… sister!"

My reaction was, "Don't touch me!!"

Having no language in which to communicate to the immigration officers, the process was easy. The immigration officer who took my passport and studied it well before he said something to his colleague in Portuguese, which I didn't understand, but they seemed in agreement. We paid for our visas, got our passports stamped, and we said the one word we'd learned in Portuguese: "Obrigado" (Thank you).

I didn't want to leave the immigration office. Afraid and not knowing how to deal with the touts outside, I took my time as if I was looking for something in my small bag. Brian noticed and teased me.

As soon as we came out, all of them stormed toward us and started fighting over who'd be taking us. Some wanted us to change money with them, some wanted us to get on their taxi. We were the only tourists at the crossing at the time, and from the look of it, not many travelers cross that border by public transport. When one of the touts who was calling me "sister" before, now grabbed my backpack and ran toward a cab, I got angry and I yelled to give me back my backpack, which offended the macho guys so that they started yelling back at me in Portuguese. I didn't care!

We had been on the road the whole day, and my patience was low. I didn't want to bargain or fight.

We took our backpacks from the touts and started walking, not knowing how long we would need to walk to find transportation or a cafe. Of course, the border was in the middle of nowhere, and it would be a long walk. As we were discussing whether we should go back to the border, we got lucky, and a Zimbabwean man with a pickup stopped for us. He introduced himself as Claver, which reminded me the funny English names we heard in Zimbabwe. He wasn't going all the way to Beira but agreed to take us to the next town, where we would be able to find some transportation or hitch a ride.

Maskarm Haile

The truth was, in northern Mozambique, there wasn't much public transportation, and even the locals had to hitchhike to move around. The scenery was breathtaking, clearly untouched by tourism or development, which meant that in some places the road was terrible. Even with our seat belts strapped on, there were times when we felt like we were jumping.

Claver dropped us off at an intersection, promising he would call and meet with us the next day. Though it felt like we had come a long way, we still had a long way to go. Once again, we stood by the roadside in a deserted village, hoping for a car to pass by so we could hitch a ride to Beira. We decided to take out our snacks and pretend we were picnicking in the middle of nowhere, chatting and reading our books. As much as not knowing whether we'd find transportation terrified us, there was also a sense of freedom. There was nothing we could do, no one to call; we had left Zimbabwe in the morning, with the help of our host, and we had depended on the kindness of strangers throughout the whole day. We were grateful how everything had worked for us so far.

When we saw a 4x4 car from afar, with only the driver in the car, we both scrambled to our feet and waved our hands. The man seemed to pass us at first but then came back. He said he was intrigued as to how we got to such an unusual place to wait for a ride. He said his name was Hasani and he was a businessman from Egypt, going to Beira.

Brian and I looked at each other. Once again, we seemed to have won the hitchhiking lottery. If it existed, this would be it!

Hasani was super-friendly, a middle-aged man who said he was having a hard time connecting with people in Northern Mozambique because he didn't speak Portuguese. His excitement in finding people to talk to was evident, and he was fascinated with the idea of us traveling overland.

Abyssinian Nomad

He volunteered to find us a reasonable hotel and take us to the beach for sunset and dinner.

As we arrived in Beira, Hasani, as promised, dropped us at the hotel he knew to be reasonable and clean. We were happy to have a roof over our head and a shower after the long day traveling.

While we waited for Hasani, I decided to go out for a little walk around the hotel where we were staying. Looking to meet locals, I tried to befriend a couple of girls who were sitting and chatting with each other. At first they seemed shy, not even looking at me, but instead glancing around to see if there was anyone with me. I was out for a walk on my own. I could see their confusion in their eyes. Though our skin color looked the same, we weren't able to communicate in words, only with the help of gestures. Desperate to make friends and to make them feel I wasn't different from them, I reluctantly agreed to let them comb and braid my hair.

The girls shyly giggled and got very excited, as if I had given them the best thing they could ever imagine. One by one they touched my hair, each saying something to the other and touching my hair again to confirm. I guess they were sure my hair was extensions; I was happy that my small gesture had broken the ice between us.

They marveled over my long, curly hair, and asked me to go bring my comb while they moved rocks for me to sit on while they combed and braided my hair. I had no idea what I'd signed up for; from experience, I knew braiding can be a long and painful process. They took some time to decide what design they wanted to braid—I could see how they debated hard to come to a decision. In the meantime, they giggled every time I asked them to be gentle when all three of them pulled my hair from different directions.

With each braid, they got louder and laughed with excitement, admiring their art, and with each braid I felt accepted and became one with the girls despite the language barrier.

Maskarm Haile

By the time Brian and Hasani came to find me, I was rocking a new hairstyle and had made new friends. I was once again excited and ready for more adventure.

Looking at the endless white sand beach in an unspoilt, remote natural wilderness was reward enough for traveling this far. The warm and clear Indian Ocean felt soft and smooth on the body as it caressed the skin. As the sun was setting and the blue sky was leaving to be replaced with a bold, vibrant orange, a deep red color took over in the sky, and it felt like it erased everything that had been dragging me around. For the first time in a long time, I was feeling light, hopeful, and just simply happy being alive.

Hasani dropped us off at the hotel after a long dinner and chat by the water, saying he'd come and meet us again tomorrow to show us more places after work. It was a day that felt like many different days in my mind, filled with so much experience. It was a collective effort that got us where we were. Each and every one of the people who'd helped us that day had contributed to my childhood dream, without even knowing it, and probably without knowing how much everything meant to me.

Though I was tired, I went to bed that night with my heart filled with gratitude.

~~~

Though Beira is the second-largest city of Mozambique, certain regions of the town seemed neglected and were slowly falling apart. One of the popular landmarks, "Casa Portugal," a house built in a typical colonial style, was in ruins, AS was the Rand Hotel near the mouth of the Rio Púngoè.

It didn't take us much to figure out it was going to be hard to explore the northern part of Mozambique without a good car. Everything we wanted to see and do was still further north, and there wasn't easily accessible public transportation. And on top of that, not being able to communicate with locals added to our frustration. As all this became clear, we wanted to leave as soon as possible.

Later in the evening, we accepted a dinner invitation from an Ethiopian family we had met earlier in South Africa. We asked if we could also invite our new friend Hasani to dinner in the hope for him to connect with new people and make friends. Mission accomplished: a small, lovely Ethiopian dinner with their beautiful baby running around, the adults chatting and debating the danger of traveling overland in Africa, marked a perfect ending for our few days' visit in the remote part of Northern Mozambique.

~~~

The next day, we once again packed our backpacks, praying we would find a ride to a highway where the trucks drove overnight to the Malawi border. Just hearing about the trucks only driving at night made my stomach flip; I'd been told lots of horror stories.

Claver, our Zimbabwean friend from the border, called us to say he knew exactly where we would find the perfect place to hitch a ride. He could come and pick us up in his truck; the only problem was he had stuff in the cab, and we'd need to sit in the back of the pickup truck.

I looked at Brian, wondering if that was a good idea.

It was our best bet, but it was the very same extremely bad road we came on to Beira, and even with seat belts we were jumping up and down inside the car. We said yes anyway, knowing at least the view would be worthwhile. On the ride, I savored feeling the wind on my face, hearing it sing, and seeing the green trees and hills around the villages. It was my most uncomfortable road trip, but being in the back gave me some kind of freedom, not only to my eyes, but to mind and heart, that made the experience worthwhile. Once we'd reached our destination, we bid our friend Claver goodbye and jumped out of the back of the truck.

As we were standing by the side of the road once again, waiting for a ride, I tried to reflect if there was anything I could have done to make the experience much more than it was. Our stay felt too short, like we didn't give Mozambique the time it required. Maybe someday I will come back; I just didn't feel good leaving a country without connecting to the place and people.

Before long a truck stopped for us, and a friendly-looking man jumped out to talk to us. We explained we wanted to go to the border. He didn't speak English well, but he understood what we were saying and agreed to give us a ride with a big smile. He even made space on his bed in the truck for me to sleep if I wanted to. It was one of those fancy, comfortable, and clean trucks, which felt very luxurious after sitting in the back of a truck on the bumpy road. There was enough space to accommodate our two backpacks and for me to lie down comfortably.

Once again, Brian and I were lucky in finding a ride, but we still didn't know how safe it was to drive at night. The roads were clearly very bad, and it was very dark. All the trucks and buses that passed by were driving like crazy. I wondered how fast they would have been driving if the roads were good. We tried to have a conversation with our new friend, we shared some food, and listened to some music. He seemed genuinely happy to have company and was curious about us. Around midnight he said he would be stopping at the next town to stretch his legs and use the toilet. He also said we would be able to find something to drink, like juice or soda. Most of the time on that trip, since one of my nightmares had been not being able to find a clean toilet, I actually embraced doing it out in the open. Actually, nature was much better than the toilets available in some places.

When we had stopped and bought soft drinks, we saw a truck drive past us. We asked why the trucks didn't slow down when they passed the villages. Our new friend said it was common practice at night for all the trucks to rush to get to the border to queue. He mentioned that we too needed to go, as sometimes the customs officials decide to do a full search and it takes a long time.

We hadn't driven that far when we saw the truck that passed us earlier had flipped over in the middle of the road. The driver almost hesitated to stop, looking worried before ultimately stopping the truck. We jumped out of the truck with our flashlights. It was the scariest thing we'd encountered, not knowing if the people in the vehicle would still be alive. We were the first to arrive, and all we could see were the shards from the shattered windscreen. We started to call out quietly at first, and then louder and louder. One of the men from inside shakily answered in Portuguese. It was a relief to see that both were alive, with minor cuts, or at least that's how it looked at the time. When we helped them get out of the truck, they said they were brothers and their eyes filled with tears, each of them happy to see the other alive. We took out our first-aid kit and tried to help them with what we had.

We gave the men our lamp and some of the antibiotic ointment. They were worried that the nearby villagers would come and steal from the truck and that it might even be dangerous for them, so they were grateful for the lamp. Our driver insisted it was time to leave, as it was getting late for him. As we were leaving, we saw a bunch of young villagers arriving with their sticks to the scene. My heart broke as we were leaving, not knowing what their fate would be in that dark, African night. Those scenes haunted me for days afterward, their look of fear replaying in my head again and again.

Chapter 14: Can We Pray for You?

"Lake Malawi is a UNESCO World Heritage Site. It's home to the largest number of fish species of any lake in the world, thought to be between 500 and 1,000."
~CNN.com

STILL TRAUMATIZED AND TIRED FROM what had happened on the road from Mozambique to Malawi, we arrived in Lilongwe early in the morning. We gave thanks to our new friend once again, and we headed to the city center to buy a SIM card, and find a cafe to sit and figure out what to do next.

Our couchsurfing host was out of town for the weekend, which left us without accommodation. It was always hard to say our exact day or time of arrival since we hitchhiked or had to depend on public transport, so it was understandable that such things could happen. While at the cafe, I also called Berhanu, an Ethiopian man. He was a friend of a friend, who lived in Lilongwe, and I was supposed to contact him when I got into town. My mother and her friends tried to connect me with people they knew who were in the countries I was visiting to make sure I would be okay, and also in case I needed anything. It was their way of knowing I was alive and safe. When I called him to inform him that we were in town and ask if he wanted to meet up later or the following day, he only asked where we were and told us to wait for him.

While we were still eating breakfast, he arrived to meet us. He was a doctor who had have been living in Malawi for some time with his family. He had heard about me and had been expecting my call. We shared our travel stories a little bit and our plans in Malawi. He heard our hitchhiking story with horror, as well as how our couchsurfing plan fell apart. He immediately decided to take us to his house, asking if we would mind staying with him, his wife and child. We didn't.

When we got to his home, his wife welcomed us as if we were some long-lost friends who'd unexpectedly showed up. Our room had been cleaned, and food and coffee were ready on the table. Their generosity was touching, and their baby was adorable. Brian couldn't figure out how Ethiopians could be so generous; they went out of their way to help and host us. It was not the first time we'd experienced Ethiopian generosity, and it wouldn't be the last. At least he received the gift graciously, even though it was hard for him to understand.

We spent the afternoon touring Lilongwe. Our host turned into a tourist guide, taking his time to show us the main attractions of the city and stopping for coffee and fresh juice along the way. We visited the war memorial, parliament building, and my favorite, the open-air market in the "Old Town." I love getting lost in open-air markets, and for me, there is no better way to experience culture and food while opening up my senses in a most profound way.

When we got back to his home, yet again there was more food cooked and waiting for us. Almaz (his wife) worried I might be feeling homesick and missing Injera (Ethiopian flat bread made of teff), so she had prepared Ethiopian food. Not only that, our laundry was washed, nicely folded, and left on our bed.

We sat around the table eating and playing with the little girl. There was lots of laughter while we shared our experiences from our travels so far. We also mentioned Brian would be leaving soon from Tanzania to go back to Canada, and I would be continuing all the way to Cairo, Egypt.

I could see and feel that piece of information made Almaz very uncomfortable and brought tears to her eyes. She studied me with love and compassion, but also wariness. While the men were talking, she told me how happy she was to have met me but that she was worried about me.

I tried to reassure her I'd be fine, even while knowing nothing on earth would make my family and friends feel at ease about this part of my journey. Before we knew it, we had created a bond, and they invited us to visit their home again on our way back from our little visit to southern Malawi.

It was a luxury to have a long hot shower and wash my hair and sleep on a comfortable, clean bed. The good night's sleep did wonders to our tired bodies and gave us another burst of energy.

~~~

The next day we rented a car and drove to Cape Maclear (Chembe), a town situated on the Nankumba Peninsula. I thought the city was quiet just because it was Sunday and most people were resting, which might be common in some African cities. But what made Lilongwe different was there was hardly any public transportation like buses or taxis. Most people walked everywhere and used bicycle taxis, sometimes mothers carrying kids or sometimes the entire family on one bicycle. I also noticed the Sunday churchgoers were in adult uniform, wearing different colored clothes with head attire. I couldn't tell which color meant which church, but it was clear the ladies in identical clothing walked together with their children, as if they were going to the same place.

Lake Malawi is the place where tourists meet culture. It's easy to see the spectacular long stretch of green emerald-like freshwater from far. Most of the accommodation is right on the water, and what makes the places special is that they aren't just reserved for tourists. The welcoming, warm, and friendly local families live around the lake. The women wake up early in the morning to do all their washing in the lake—clothes, dishes, their kids and themselves, while their dogs and the cattle drink near where they wash.

My favorite experience at Lake Malawi was a day trip by traditional boat to go snorkeling and have lunch at the Lake Malawi National Park, where we saw a variety of colorful tropical fish in their natural habitat. It was also a treat to see the fish eagles so close, diving in and out of the water so often. Just floating around in the calm, warm, clear lake comforted both my body and mind.

When we came back to Lilongwe one last time, once again there was a feast prepared for us, with traditional Ethiopian coffee, and our laundry had been done. I could feel our host's wife's desperation, worry, and the desire to keep me safe, but she didn't know how. She reminded me of my mother. She was clearly dreading the moment we had to leave. She was almost in tears and did the only thing she knew how to do, and that was to hand me over to her god. She asked if they could pray for us. We said yes, and we all held hands and prayed.

At that moment, I realized how much pain and worry I sometimes inflicted on people unintentionally, just because I wanted to follow my heart and do things most people from my culture didn't know were possible, or simply didn't think were necessary, or just considered plain crazy.

Maskarm Haile

I could see by the look in their eyes how helpless many people felt when confronted with my unusual lifestyle, and that they were lost in thoughts, trying to determine my sanity. Some went to the extent to say there was a devil inside me that made me do things like this, and all I needed was holy water to fix it. And in some cases, they blamed Brian and Canada for how I turned out as a woman. I saw their struggle to understand me, to try to open their minds and look interested in what I say, but their words failing them.

Sometimes I feel I am going around and disturbing the peace of others, shattering their belief systems, and making them question their own lives. Though my intention and promise to myself is to be open, to learn and share, I see the discomfort it creates in people's lives when they hear my stories. I have had experiences where I talk about my travels with a complete stranger, and I have witnessed them going to a distant place within themselves, trying to keep up with my story, but also diving into their own world. They hear my voice but are not listening; they nod and smile, but don't look into my eyes. Most of the time what happens after that is magical. I wait. I have come to understand everything isn't about me.

Then they start telling me about the dreams they have had or the things they wanted to do. But it's more than that: they are downloading something from that deep place and giving it sounds, words, textures, and feelings while sharing their stories. I get a chill up and down my spine; sometimes we both feel something that can't be explained in words, we recognize something special has taken place. I give my gratitude to the universe because I have come to understand it is one of the vital experiences I seek in my existence, and connecting with people feels so good.

At the start of my traveling path, I didn't want to let go of the people, and there was a lot of suffering that came from that desire. Now I understand there is no need to worry where such a connection will take place, nor with what kind of person, be it man, woman, young or old; sometimes that connection can only happen when we are not able to talk because of the language barrier.

I have seen this connection happen more than few times, and I have come to love, accept, and honor it when it takes place. I also long and crave that kind of free-flowing connection with fellow human beings when I'm not traveling. It's mostly the reason why I need a plane ticket to somewhere, anywhere, to fulfill that desire.

As we were close to the end of our stay in Malawi, Brian bought his return ticket to Cape Town, to connect to his flight back to Europe and Canada. And that is when I started to feel something within me shutting down. One more country and Brian would be flying out. Nothing in me felt ready for the separation, but I couldn't bring myself to ask him questions. It was eating me alive. I also resented him; I resented the fact that by allowing him to come along, I allowed such a situation to happen. I resented the fact that I didn't know what I wanted, and I also knew it probably wasn't a good time to make a big life decision when I was feeling so desperate for love, and wanting to be understood, accepted, kept safe, and guided by someone strong.

It was one of the worst times of my life, but I was also in love. I had loved Brian for the last four years. There were just too many memories we had created together, and I couldn't look at most of my photo albums without being reminded of what it was like to be with him. I was so tired of waiting for something to change, and I couldn't seem to summon up enough courage and willpower to let go.

Chapter 15: Badly Proposed

"The Ngorongoro Crater is home to the world's densest population of lions, wildebeest, elephants, hippopotamus, rhinoceros, zebra, leopards, and hyenas. There are approximately 25,000 animals in the crater of just 100 square miles. That's 250 animals per mile."
~ 20 facts about Tanzania

WE GOT TRANSPORTATION TO THE border of Tanzania and took a crazy taxi ride to Mbeya. We had wanted to take the Tazara train from Mbeya to Dar es Salaam. According to the Lonely Planet Guidebook we had, we were late for the train, but that guidebook had been wrong most of the time on our journey, so we decided to go and check out the train station ourselves.

The taxi driver, who drove like crazy, also confirmed the train hadn't yet passed. Mbeya is a charming mountain town, but there wasn't enough to do there until the next train came a few days later. When we arrived at the station it was almost empty, and we thought we had missed the train, but when we approached the counter, we were told the train was delayed and we could still buy tickets for it.

Abyssinian Nomad

It was supposed to be one of the best African train rides through the mountains and national parks. But there was one problem: apart from not speaking Swahili, we found out with the help of our taxi driver that we couldn't be in the same cabin even if we bought first-class tickets, since the cabins for men and women were segregated. Even married couples couldn't share unless they bought the entire cabin for themselves. That would mean a twenty-four-hour train ride in separate sections... Luckily, there was an entire first-class sleeping cabin available.

The decision was made. We bought the tickets and waited impatiently for the train to arrive. The first thing I noticed was how calm Tanzanians were. The train was delayed for more than three hours, and there was no one out to advise the new passengers or to give a new arrival time. Every time we approached the counter to ask if they had a new estimated time of arrival, they looked at us as if something was wrong with us for being impatient. It seemed they were feeling sorry for us, as they were saying, "Pole, pole," which means "slowly, slowly" in Swahili.

The Tazara train is notorious for being late most of the time. Once on the train, we didn't care how long it took for us to get to Dar es Salaam. We were well prepared with books, magazines, and snacks, and as promised, there was a dining car with a variety of food, coffee, and drinks. The train also stopped in some small towns where passengers got on and off the train while vendors sold cold water, colorful fruits, fresh hapatti, and other local snacks.

Gliding through lush green mountains and small villages, we lay on our bed and watched in awe. It was one of those surreal moments worth every bit of trouble we went through to get there. Finally, we fell asleep, and when we woke up, the scenery had changed, and it was getting warmer. But we still had time to watch elephants and zebras as we were crossing Mikumi National Park.

Maskarm Haile

The twenty-four-hour train ride turned into almost forty-eight hours with lots of delays, but I was so elated that I had even forgotten Tanzania was the country from which Brian would be leaving. It was as if my heart and mind couldn't deal with all the challenges I was facing, so I tuned them out. At that very moment, I felt fully alive, vibrant, and ecstatically happy. There was no other place I wanted to be, nothing I wanted to do except lie in that cabin, and read my book occasionally staring outside the window.

This was a change from how I usually felt. I was kind of anxious about finding transport or crossing borders before. I had come a long way on my journey through Africa. I was almost halfway, and that was a milestone for me. I observed and marveled at every experience, with gratitude deep inside me. I looked at Brian and felt a sense of relief. Whatever his reason for being there, I believed the experience had made him happy. But the one thing I was even more grateful for was that nothing bad had happened to him, or to us, apart from the car breaking down, a couple of flat tires, and that big venomous snake in Namibia that we'd found in the spa. No matter what I told myself, I felt responsible for his presence in Africa at that particular time. That we had reached Tanzania safely meant one of my biggest prayers was being answered.

It was late in the afternoon when the train finally arrived in Dar es Salaam. We were exhausted, covered in dust, and had no idea where we were going to spend the night. The guidebook suggested how to get to Zanzibar after the train ride, but the last ferry had already left, and the last plane was also leaving soon. As the guidebook had mentioned, some touts sold tickets for Zanzibar. It was true: a man came, confidently telling us he would get us on the last small plane if we quickly followed him. Brian hesitated, but me, I didn't want to have to find a place for one night only and then travel all over again in the morning to get to Zanzibar. I just wanted to get to

Zanzibar, unpack, take a nice shower, and not worry about waking up early in the morning to catch a ferry or plane. We piled our backpacks in the small taxi and headed to the airport, following the man. We didn't know who he was or how he managed to do it, but he did get us on the last Coastal Aviation flight to Zanzibar.

We paid for the tickets, but weren't even issued any. All I remember was we did a lot of running. I was not even sure if our luggage was screened—the man ahead of us had carried my backpack because I couldn't run carrying it—but I remember seeing our packs being loaded onto the small plane, and then we boarded the aircraft. I looked at Brian with satisfaction and thanked him for agreeing to catch the last-minute flight rather than wait until the next day. It was a short flight, twenty minutes, and we were there before we knew it. All my tiredness was gone, and my heart sang. We had identified a few hostels where we could stay in Stone Town, Zanzibar's capital, but we had no idea if they had available rooms. We took a taxi and just showed up.

Zanzibar is the largest island of an archipelago. It has a truly breathtaking palm-fringed coastline that goes for miles, disappearing into an aqua ocean. Its long heritage of blended culture and lively history and its unique mixture of architectural styles – Arabic, Indian, European, Persian and African—give it exotic feel. I instantly fell in love with Zanzibar, and it felt oddly familiar. Everything I smelled, felt, touched, saw, ate, and heard brought so much joy within me that I could hardly contain myself. I didn't understand a word of Swahili, but even that sound was so beautiful in my ears. As we walked through the labyrinth of Stone Town streets too narrow for cars to pass, smiling and greeting shop vendors who sold everything from sand to oils, and anything in between, my heart sang and my spirit soared in a way I'd never experienced before.

Maskarm Haile

Everything felt alive, true, and simply beautiful.

The friendly staff at the hostel in Stone Town booked us an eco and cultural tour to visit the popular spice farm, saying the history of Zanzibar would be incomplete without the nutmeg, cloves, cinnamon, vanilla, pepper, and many other spices which are essential ingredients of Zanzibaris' daily life. Growing up in Ethiopia, one of my favorite things was drinking tea with cinnamon, cardamom, and cloves, a very common practice. But I never knew what they looked like fresh or as plants. I was already super-excited.

A bus that picked us up from our hostel was filled with enthusiastic and friendly tourists, with whom we talked to and got to know a bit on our spice farm walk. The tour guide explained how spices and herbs were originally introduced to Zanzibar by Portuguese traders in the 16th century, brought from their colonies in South America and India. Simply walking on the farm alone, one can smell the strong aroma of fresh spices. Tasting and touching the different spices and tropical exotic fruits takes the taste buds to a different level. Not only that, there was an unlimited amount of fresh coconut water that quenched our thirst and kept us hydrated.

The tour included a Swahili lunch with lots of flavorful rice and sauces, and vegetables, and fruits that tasted and smelled so much better than any I have ever eaten.

After lunch and a long conversation about food, culture, and spices in Zanzibar, the tour guide informed us we had about two hours to explore the deserted white sand beach outside town. Once there, every one of us jumped in the warm and clear Indian Ocean to cool off from the heat. A couple of us had already bonded, and we stuck together to chat more as we were floating in the ocean. The question for all of us was what brought us to Zanzibar. As everyone in turn said they were visiting Tanzania or East Africa, I started reflecting about my own answer. I wasn't in Zanzibar just because I'd read about it in the guidebook—my journey had started years ago, when I befriended a Zanzibari schoolmate in India who constantly talked about Zanzibar being a paradise. But I didn't say all that; I simply smiled and said I was on a journey from Cape to Cairo. Which brought a few eyebrows up. And suddenly one of the American tourists joked, saying why was I swimming in the ocean with them? She said she didn't recall Ethiopians being known for swimming, but for long-distance running.

To which I answered, "I guess there is a first time for everything, eh?" To which we all agreed before coming out of the water into the scorching sun again.

The next few days, Brian and I aimlessly walked around Stone Town, ate at the food market in the evening, drank endless coconut water and took a boat to Changuu (Prison Island), where we snorkeled and played with the big tortoises.

It was the best way to end my trip with Brian, I thought!

~~~

We took the ferry back to Dar es Salaam. I felt sick knowing it was time for Brian to leave, but something hit me hard when we got to Dar es Salaam. I was done living with the uncertainty of our relationship.

Once again, we met up with a family friend, Nebiu, who was working in Dar es Salaam. It was a nice distraction—we went out for a sushi dinner with his family, and it was fun again meeting new people and hanging out. He offered to connect me with his friend in Arusha to host me after Dar es Salaam. We talked about Brian's departure, without me showing my fear and anxiety.

I'd also sent a couch request to a local couchsurfer, Dominque, asking him if I could stay with him and his family for a couple of days in Dar es Salaam after Brian left.

Maskarm Haile

Dominque, the young Tanzanian who was living with his brother and sisters close to the biggest open market, Kariakoo, was willing to host me, and I was happy about it. Kariakoo is considered one of the most dangerous areas in town but it was my first local host, and I wasn't going to pass up the opportunity to stay with a local family.

The night before Brian's departure, I started to get very sick. I guess my body couldn't take my emotional stress anymore. I cried so much; it was as if heaven's floodgates opened up inside me. Brian was quick to suggest that he would come with me all the way to Cairo—he wanted to travel with me. Though that sounded good, but I wasn't looking for a quick fix; I wanted way more than traveling to Cairo. I wanted him to commit to me and say we'd have a happily-ever-after. I didn't want to go back to Ethiopia with him when I couldn't tell my family what they wanted to hear, which was that we were to be engaged or married.

I found the courage to speak what was on my mind, even though it made me physically ill and I almost wanted to die. I had been running away from commitment most of my life, and there I was offering myself to a man who was not ready to commit. I had reached rock bottom.

I had a high fever and began to throw up. I was feeling fragile, and both of us were crying; neither of us thought that separating again would be this hard. It was late and completely dark outside, so it was not possible for us to go out for a walk. Besides, Dar es Salaam isn't known for its safety record. I stayed in bed, apart from having to run to the bathroom every so often to throw up.

At some point in the night, Brian proposed to me, saying he loved me and wanted to be with me. For a moment, I thought I hadn't heard him correctly.

I said yes.

We kissed, wiping each other's tears and declaring our love for each other. We made passionate love, but when it was all over, I don't think either of us slept for the rest of the night.

I wanted to be happy about the news; I tried to be happy! Wasn't this what I had been waiting for? A glimpse of a possible future with Brian? And if it was what I wanted, why didn't I feel happy? But something within me had died, and I was still sick. When I woke up from my short, restless sleep, I expected Brian to say what happened the previous night was all a mistake, and he was going to get on that plane. But he didn't!

How was it possible that the one thing I had wanted so much, didn't feel right? I was still feeling weak, tired and sick. But I couldn't stay in bed; we had to check out of the hotel.

While packing up my backpack, I gathered my courage once again to ask if he was coming to my couchsurfing host with me, though what I really wanted to ask Brian was whether he remembered what he had said to me the night before or if he could repeat those words so I could believe them. Because right then, I didn't believe any of it. None of it felt real or true in my heart and soul. It's not that I didn't *want* to believe him, but I knew for sure that wasn't how I was supposed to feel. It felt like more of a death sentence to my soul rather than a happy marriage proposal.

I called my Tanzanian host Dominque to ask if I could take Brian along with me. He said yes, and told me a place and time to meet him, and we navigated the crowded market area for the first time on rickshaw. (A local three-wheel transport). Our Tanzanian host and his family lived in a two-bedroom modest house. Our stay with the young family touched our hearts, but it also put things in perspective for me. The older brother, who was the couchsurfer, was a young man who brought his sisters and brothers from a remote village where his family lives, so they could get an education. He was going to school and working full time to support his family.

Not only that, but he also hosted couchsurfers whenever he could. We spent two nights with them, going to the market and sightseeing. It was both fun and a distraction; it took away the pain I was feeling deep inside me. Over homemade dinner (Ugali, beans and fried plantain), the brothers and sisters asked if I have family. I wasn't sure if they were asking me about my parents and sisters or if I have my own family, but I answered that my family is in Ethiopia.

Seeming even more confused, they asked if I had permission from my father to travel. I said I was old enough and didn't need permission, but I did have my family's blessing. Again that didn't seem easy for them to understand.

As the elder brother took out his laptop and started to explain my extensive traveling, showing them my couchsurfing profile and world map, it dawned on him that his family had never hosted a couchsurfer who looked like them. They'd hosted non-Africans for so long, the kids were convinced all travelers must be non-African. We all laughed about that revelation.

But then as we were about to gather the plates and food from the table, one of his shy sisters came toward me and, in a slow voice, said she wanted to travel like me when she grows up. My heart melted hearing her words, and when everyone asked what she said to me, she didn't want to say. So I told her she didn't have to worry—it was going to be our secret.

We took an early bus to Arusha, where the Rwandan Genocide Tribune Court was installed, and there were lots of United Nations workers. Once again, a family friend welcomed us. She came to pick us up from the bus station and took us to her house. By that time Brian had given up asking me how these arrangements worked. The last comment he made in Dar was that he didn't know what was with the Ethiopians, as no Canadian would take him home just because he was Canadian unless he desperately needed help.

We spent a few days exploring the area, but not talking much. When Brian asked me if I had told my family about our engagement, I was not able to answer. Usually, when people are happy they share their happiness. And it's not that I didn't talk to my mother. I had been calling my mom every day because I worried her energy level was going down. And me, I was feeling…

No, I didn't even know what I was feeling. I had had such a hard time those past few weeks that I didn't know what I felt about anything anymore.

The silence was killing me. We took a shuttle from Arusha to Nairobi, Kenya. Because of a major road construction, the shuttle took more than six hours, including a stop at the Kenyan border crossing for a visa and a quick stop at the restaurant. While we were passing through small villages, mountains, and towns, getting closer to the big city, it was clear Brian and I were growing apart. We hardly said anything to each other, both of us lost in our thoughts.

It was in that uncomfortable mini bus, on a rough and dusty road, with probably the craziest driver I was yet to experience, and most of our fellow passengers wondering if we were going to make it to Nairobi alive, that I found my answer to my burning question.

Chapter 16: Chilling Truth

"Truth is like fire it cannot be hidden under dry leaves."
~ African Proverb

The country is named after Mt. Kenya, which is the highest point in the country and is 17,057 feet high.
~ 50 Amazing facts about Kenya

WHEN WE GOT TO NAIROBI, we headed to East Gate, where we were supposed to meet our couchsurfing host at the Cafe Java. I was physically exhausted, and the grey sky outside made me feel emotionally drained. But somehow Nairobi unexpectedly comforted me. I guess being in a familiar place and getting a good coffee helped.

I was not sure how we started the conversation, but I seem to remember that Brian said something like it wasn't working. I neither agreed with him nor said anything else. I was just too tired to think. Too tired of everything! I felt like I had been holding my breath for a long time. I looked out the window, and the rain had started pouring. I heard Brian saying that even the sky was crying for us. For me, the rain was a perfect expression of my innermost feelings. The rain said what I couldn't.

My phone rang, and it was our host. He was on his way from work and coming to pick us up. I wasn't sure if Brian was still coming with me. I looked at Brian, and he said he was going to come with me and book a flight to Cairo that would leave within the next few days.

The peak rush-hour traffic in Nairobi was horrible, and on top of that it was a Friday evening, and it was raining. It was just pure misery. But our host, a young Thai man who was working in Nairobi, was super-warm and friendly. He mentioned he was invited to a birthday party and said we were welcome to join if we wanted. Politely, I declined. All I wanted was a shower and a long sleep. I had had a long day. After dropping us at his house, he quickly showed us around and left, giving us his house key in case we changed our minds and wanted to go out. I was touched by his action because not many people in Nairobi give their house keys to someone they've just met. He trusted us and left us alone in his apartment.

I was feeling sick again, but I didn't tell Brian. All I wanted was a hot shower. Luckily, our host was living in a beautiful hotel apartment that had incredible, hot, running water. I stripped off my dusty clothes, stepped into the shower, pressed my head against the smooth shower wall, and let the water wash over me. Not only did I want to wash the dust out of my hair and off my body, but I also wanted to cleanse my soul. I felt the hot steam release the tension and aches from my body, but the water wasn't able to loosen the heartache I was holding inside.

No tears came. I was done. I couldn't even cry anymore.

I was so tired I fell asleep before Brian even finished his shower. The sleeping arrangement was perfect: for the first time, it was an actual couch, so Brian and I didn't have to share a bed.

Maskarm Haile

In the morning, I woke from a horrible dream and couldn't remember what it was about. When our host suggested we go out grocery shopping to buy the ingredients for breakfast, I was happy, though all I wanted was coffee!

Seeing me so tired and weak, Brian suggested we also buy a pregnancy test, just in case. It hadn't even crossed my mind that I could be pregnant. In a split second, a million things went through my mind, and I felt even sicker, if that was possible. But I couldn't show my host or Brian that I was sick. The last thing I wanted was to be a burden. Once we were outside, the cold air helped, and I waited for them at the cafe while they did the shopping.

In the meantime, I tried to call my mother, just to hear her comforting voice. But she didn't answer her phone. I kept on trying and then finally, in a panic I called my sister.

As my sister answered her phone, I heard something, a kind of hesitation in her voice and got even more worried about my mother. Because I couldn't tell my sister what I was really feeling without falling apart, I started talking very fast. I told her I was in Nairobi and said that I would have to stay there for a while until I got a new passport. There were only two pages left in my passport, and I needed to apply for a new one. The Canadian Embassy in Nairobi said it would take two to three weeks. I was considering going to Ethiopia and applying from there, but that would mean it would take longer since they would have to send my passport to Nairobi first and then to Canada.

My sister started to say something again, but her voice was unsteady, so I blurted out my question: "Is Mommy okay? Why is she not answering her calls?" My sister paused for a second and said that our mother was frail and could hardly talk. My sister was hesitating to tell me, because our mother had told her not to. I don't remember what I said to my sister after that or how I ended our conversation. I hung up the phone; it felt like I had fallen into a bottomless hole, and would never find my way out.

When Brian and our host came back, I told them the news.

Brian and I booked our flights together for the next day. Our departure appeared to be divinely coordinated: our flights were a few minutes apart, departing from the same airport. To my great relief, the pregnancy test was negative.

~~~

Knowing what I know now, there was nothing to say and no tears to shed for our relationship. The truth was I loved Brian, and I was desperate, and didn't want to lose him. I loved him because he is a good, good man, he brought out the playful child in me, but more than, that he allowed me to be who I want to be. He never said to me, "you shouldn't" or "you can't." I have a video he took of me while bungee jumping, and when we watched the video, I saw the camera was shaking. I didn't have to ask him why—I knew. He believed in my crazy ideas and supported me every time, even if it scared him to death. Even if his hands shook watching me taking that leap of faith.

Of course, I had every reason to want to hold on to this man. I didn't want him to leave me, especially not when my mother was fighting for her own life. But there was also a truth that dawned on me: as much as I wanted Brian and didn't want to let him go, Brian and I were not friends. We didn't have a deep connection and communication. We were both emotionally bankrupt people who didn't really say much when things got tough.

Though it was painful, we gave each other a quick hug and went our separate ways. Brian went to Cairo, Egypt, and I went to Addis Ababa, Ethiopia.

Maskarm Haile

I was lost in my thoughts when my flight was called for boarding. I was mostly worried about my mother, and wondering about my life too, I guess. Wondering where I should start when everything I knew had fallen apart. I felt as if I was standing on a mountain of sand and the sand was sliding from under my feet.

My goal was simple: to stay standing, to not slip because, God forbid, if I did, I would never know how to get up again.

Chapter 17: The Biggest Loss of My Life

"I hope you never hear those words. Your mom. She died. They are different than other words. They are too big to fit in your ears. They belong to some strange, heavy, powerful language that pounds away at the side of your head, a wrecking ball coming at you again and again, until finally, the words crack a hole large enough to fit inside your brain. And in so doing, they split you apart."
~ Mitch Albom

I THOUGHT I HAD EXPERIENCED loss in 2003, when I was traveling in the Maritimes, and woke up one morning to find an email that told me my small apartment in Montreal with everything I owned—I mean everything that had my past, present and possible future, like years of journaling, picture albums, documents, computer, books, etc.—was burned to the ground and I didn't have a place to go back to. If that weren't enough, my short-lived engagement ended the very same week. A friend had suggested I read Pema Chodron's book, *When Things Fall Apart*. I read and reread the wonderful book and found some insight that made me understand how to move forward from my situation. But the worst things that had happened in my life, I thought, never compared to where I was and what I felt on that short flight back to Addis Ababa, Ethiopia, from Nairobi, Kenya.

A longtime friend who was very close to my family was picking me up from the airport. I had already told my sister I was coming, but we didn't tell my mother. She was in the hospital.

In my head, I started to dread the questions I would have to face from family members and friends who'd be coming to visit Mom again:

"You have lost weight!"

"You are darker." (Mind you, I have never really been light-skinned.)

"What happened to your hair?"

"What are you wearing?"

All those questions were thrown at me before I was asked how I was, or we'd even finished the obligatory three kisses on a cheek. A long time ago, I used to try to justify the changes, but now, I tried not to let those questions get to me or to say things that would offend anyone.

To everyone's surprise, I showed up at the hospital unannounced. My mother was pleasantly surprised, happy, and even relieved in some way. She asked if my sister had told me to come. I didn't want her to think we were worried, so I told her about running out of pages in my passport and needing a new one. I thought I could apply for a new one in Addis, and since it was going to take a few weeks, I'd hang out with her and the family in Addis. Knowing I was going to be around for a few weeks made her happy.

The next question was the one I dreaded the most. My mother asked how Brian was and where he was. Because everything had happened so fast, I hadn't thought about how I would deal with that question. I knew he would probably call me again from Cairo to ask about her, so I just said he flew to Cairo. It was understandable that he couldn't sit and wait for me until I got my new passport.

Truthfully, I just wanted to make it easy for her. There was no way I wanted her to worry about me. I immediately understood the seriousness of her situation. She was fragile, and could hardly eat, sit, or talk. The doctors and nurses came and went. I noticed from my last experience in the hospital with her how they controlled the hospital. How they stormed into the room unannounced and told everyone to leave whenever they wished. They could also be extremely rude to the caregivers. I know knowledge is power, but it can only be misused in a place like Ethiopia, where the majority of the population is uneducated.

I understood they needed to do their job, but knowing how hard it was for the caregivers, I was disappointed to witness how the medical staff treated people. Sometimes after the doctors' rounds, they just left without explaining what was going on with the patient. Of course, the nurses made sure everyone had left the room before the doctor walked in, as if he or she was God and needed to be worshiped from afar. I didn't like any of that, and I refused to accept their behavior.

I needed to tackle the issue without getting overly confrontational with them when they walked in. I tried to get to know the nurses who attended to my mother and formally introduced myself to her doctor. In front of my mom, I politely but firmly explained I wanted to know everything that was going on. That meant I was not leaving the room when they came, and they would not leave the room without answering my questions or anyone's questions. I didn't expect them to take that with smiles and friendly handshakes, but I stood my ground.

The next week was a roller-coaster ride. One day my mother was okay and the next very sick. If anyone has experienced caring for a sick loved one, they will know what I'm talking about. One day, I was hopeful, and the next day I was lost and desperate. My sisters and I stayed with her, only leaving her side to take a shower and eat when she had visitors. Once again, I got a chance to see most of our relative and family friends that I hadn't seen in a long time. It was comforting and heartwarming how they made time to come and wish her well.

I noticed my mother had visitors from different churches and monasteries too. There were mostly monks who knew about each one of us, her children. I certainly didn't know most of them, but these monks knew my name (my Christian baptism name), and as my mother had asked them all those years ago, they had been praying for me over the years. No wonder I was still alive.

It was overwhelming to know all these people I'd never met before had been praying for me, and probably my mother too, for all these years. It was very comforting to know that.

I had come a long way since her first diagnosis four years back. I had had time to play the victim, feel angry, sad, heartbroken, confused and scared. Through the process, there were moments when I had felt hopeful, embracing, honoring, optimistic, but at other times, I didn't know what I was experiencing. I was not even sure what I was supposed to feel or not feel.

According to Elisabeth Kübler-Ross, a Swiss-American psychiatrist, a pioneer in near-death studies, and the author of the groundbreaking book, *On Death and Dying*, we go through five stages of grief and loss:

1. Denial and Isolation
2. Anger
3. Bargaining
4. Depression
5. Acceptance

Abyssinian Nomad

We do not necessarily go through them in that order or even experience all five stages. But I had gone through all of them. It had even felt like I had gone through more stages. Now, I felt like I was back at the bargaining stage.

~~~

I was introduced to the reincarnation concept while living in India, but I had no idea where I stood with that information for years. Death is not a secret in India as it was in Ethiopia. The dead bodies were paraded on the streets openly, whereas, in Ethiopia, not even family members get to see the body.

But then Rebecca, an Ethiopian artist I met in Cotonu, Benin, lent me a book that entirely changed the way I understood death and afterlife: *Many Lives, Many Masters,* by a traditional psychotherapist, Dr. Brian Weiss. The book is a detailed account of the events that transformed Dr. Weiss from a skeptic into a firm believer in reincarnation.

The idea was new to me, but that didn't make it bad or good. I didn't have to believe in anything right away, but could be open to new learning, and understanding the nature of things. But my mother was different; she didn't like death, and didn't like to talk about the death of others, let alone her own death. I never asked her why, but every time the subject came up, her energy shifted. So I left it alone, not wanting to distress her.

While rereading the book and discussing it with Rebecca, I mentioned the resentment I felt about losing my friends and my grandmother at an early age. That was when Rebecca shared her deep, insightful story about the night her mother passed. A story that profoundly touched my heart and changed me forever. She said her sisters and brothers had gathered from around the world to be by their mother's side for the last time. All were adults, with different backgrounds and belief systems.

Maskarm Haile

"We have a choice about death," she said. "The choice was either to cry and blame God, or take the time to say goodbye in private while comforting our mother in her transition and comforting each other for the new, unknown life; a life without her."

Rebecca told me that beautiful story as if she was narrating a book. At that time, I couldn't even conceive of the idea of my mother being sick, let alone dying. But now, I couldn't help but remember the story Rebecca had shared with me, as I sat in the hospital room watching my mother going in and out of consciousness. I told myself that I had a choice. It was not the choice I wanted to have, but it was a choice at least, something I could make use of. The story I'd heard in 2002 from a random Ethiopian woman in Benin would help me find my own courage and make my own decisions about the next few hours of my mother's life. I will be forever grateful to Rebecca for sharing her story.

The doctors came and left; my mother slipped between consciousness and unconsciousness while I sat there and watched. But every time she opened her eyes she smiled at us, not wanting us to worry, I assume. But it was clear she needed more morphine, and her organs were shutting down one by one. My younger sister Selam, the third in the family, and I sat on each side of the bed holding each other's hands. My sister looked at me as if I had answers for what was happening. We both felt helpless and defeated.

None of us dared to leave the room. The family came to give us a break, trying to get us to go out for a walk or eat something. My other sister called. I didn't want to believe what my inner voice was saying about my mother. So, I ignored it. I kept myself busy thinking about other things, and my sister called again. She asked me the usual question: "How's Mommy? What did the doctors say? Does she need anything?"

Abyssinian Nomad

And then I blurted out, as if I were translating something for my sister: "I am going to say this only once, so listen! If you want to see her alive, take the next plane and come. If not, please don't call me again. Because I have to go out of the room each time I have to answer the phone, and I don't want to leave my mother's bedside anymore."

Selam and I sat at her bedside, looking at each other every now and then, knowing our world was collapsing and there was nothing we could do about it. Life would never be the same again. A little later my other sister called again to say the next available flight was the following day or two days later. I told her it would be too late and hung up the phone.

Two days before that, my mother was feeling suddenly awake and energized and was talking to her longtime friend Tutu, who happened to be visiting her with some traditional Ethiopian food. I ate that meal alone with my mom, since it was a fasting season in Ethiopia and no one else was eating dairy products. Did I know that would be my last meal with my mother? No.

I wonder if everyone in the family would have shared the meal if they'd known it would be the last one? That was the last time I spoke to and saw my mother awake. After that the situation changed. My mother's organs started to fail one by one, and all the doctor could do was give her morphine so she didn't suffer. They were professional and courteous when they communicated with us. My sister and I just sat there and listened.

My phone rang again, and it was my other sister, this time saying she was on her way to the airport and had given her flight details so a friend could pick her up. I went inside the hospital room. With some part of me pleading, some part asking, and some part demanding, I said to my mother,

"Your daughter is on the way, and I was the one who forced her to come today, so you better be here when she gets here. I promised her you will be alive, so you need to stay. You need to stay for her, you need to stay for me, you need to stay…" I cried.

Of course, I wasn't expecting an answer, but I knew she heard me. And I knew she would keep my promise. But the day felt like an eternity. The doctor was often there to give her more morphine, and it was the most painful thing I'd ever had to witness. I felt tremendously guilty for holding my mother hostage when she was suffering so much, but I also thought my sister wouldn't have forgiven me if I hadn't told her the truth.

My sister and I sat on either side of my mother, each of us holding her hand. Occasionally some visitors or family members came in and went away. I saw some of them whispering to each other, and suddenly someone disappeared and came back. It seemed as if we also had a lot more visitors so they could say their goodbyes. As much as I didn't want to believe that voice within me, it was that voice that made me tell my sister to come, and she was on her way. So maybe her friends and family heard a similar voice, as they were there to say goodbye.

I felt broken into pieces. Brian called me a few times, and each time I spoke to him, I cried. I had to run with the phone so no one would see me crying—it wasn't the time for that yet. I couldn't afford to fall apart, not then, and not later, because I didn't have anyone to pick me up and piece me together anymore. Every so often, I said to my mother that my sister was on her way, and she couldn't go yet. It became my mantra, as if she needed a reminder.

Just before midnight, my sister walked in. After looking at our mother unconscious, she ran out, stifling her cries. I gave my thanks to my mother, I told her how much I loved her and set her free from my side. I thanked her for waiting for my sister, I thanked her for everything she had given me and everyone who crossed her path, I thanked her for trusting me.

At that moment, the nurse came around and told everyone to leave.

But my sister Selam and I refused to leave the room, sitting and holding our mother's hands and each other's hands. My eyes were fixed on my mother's face, her eyes and her breathing. Then just like that, she took her last breath. It was peaceful, almost like witnessing a miracle. It felt like everything stopped for a moment. Even as she was taking her final breath, my mother taught me a profound lesson in life. At that moment, I was aware that my breath was the only thing that separated me from my dead mother. That thing I often take for granted was showing me the power it held in my life. I was fully present in my body, to the experience, but I heard someone crying and screaming outside.

The nurses came hurrying into the room and told my sister and me to leave the room immediately, promising they would let us in again later. They said they needed to resuscitate my mother; it didn't make sense, but to avoid argument, I agreed and walked out. My sister asked me something, but I couldn't look at her. If I had, I would have broken down, and it was not the time for that. I fought my way through the room once again, and my sister followed me. I guessed they thought we would make a scene by screaming and crying in the hospital room and disturb others, but we didn't say anything; as calm as we could be, we kissed our mother, and we left the room. I heard some of them saying how wrong it was for us to have kissed her. Apparently, no one was supposed to kiss a dead body, because of some kind of superstition.

I don't remember much about the next few days—I was on autopilot. My sisters and I were confronted by the new reality of making a decision just a few hours after losing our mother. The adults gathered around us and told us there was conflict in the family about where our mother was going to be buried. I couldn't believe that my mother hadn't planned her burial. I knew about her fear of death, but I didn't think that decision should have been left to us, especially as it was so important in her belief system.

I would have swapped places with my mother a million times rather than having to make the decision about where she should be buried. My uncle, my mother's older brother Getachew, thought she should be buried in a monastery outside Addis Ababa, where their mother had been buried. He reasoned that the place was holy and if she were buried there, she would go to heaven. Our father wanted her to be buried at St. Michael's church in the city, where she often went to service, and we could easily go to visit. But there was one problem with that idea: there was not enough land, and her casket would have to be buried in a mausoleum wall vault, a no-no for some religious people.

I was sure my sisters and I were looking at practicality more than anything else. I also didn't believe my mother's afterlife was determined by where she was buried. I am someone who lives my life honoring my heaven and hell right here on earth. But I was not going to argue the point. Yet while all these discussions were happening in the early morning, with my siblings and I crammed in one corner of the house and my father and a few other people outside, our uncle came in with our family priest. Out of nowhere, we were asked to have another meeting.

I hadn't seen the priest in a long time, and I remembered how much our parents loved and respected him. I was happy to see him and thought for a second he would offer a little comfort. However, the words that came out of his mouth were devastating. He lectured us, including my father, saying we were irresponsible and not worthy of our mother. I wanted to scream, wondering if it was that important, why had they neglected to ask her what she wanted before she died, and then blamed us afterward. But by then I had put my foot down and agreed with my father, thinking that at least I could visit her grave whenever I was in town. My sisters also sided with our father. The priest and our uncle stormed out of our house, cursing us.

My first reaction was shock that those people loved my mother and respected her so much for as long as I had known them, but hours, not days or months, but hours after her death, they came to our house and cursed her husband and children because of our choices. I realized right then how much our mother had protected us, and though we were all adults, we had never dealt with serious family stuff. For the next few days, family, friends, and people we didn't know came to the house to help with everything, while I sat in a corner and witnessed what community living was all about. It was for this day that my family had made sure they signed up to the Edir.

"*Edir*—*In Ethiopia, an Edir (var. eddir, idir) is a traditional community organization whose members assist each other during the mourning process. Members make monthly financial contributions forming the Edir's fund. They are entitled to receive a certain sum of money from this fund to help cover funeral and other expenses associated with deaths. Additionally, Edir members comfort the mourners: female members take turns doing housework, such as preparing food for the mourning family, while male members usually take the responsibility to arrange the funeral and erect a temporary tent to shelter guests who come to visit the mourning family. Edir members are required to stay with the mourning family and comfort them for three full days.*[4]"

Though I had a different approach to life, I was genuinely grateful and amazed how much every one of them gave their time, energy, and money every day. Everyone dealt with the task at hand: you were kept busy and avoided the pain inside. People would come and talk to us to try to make us forget our loss, at least for that moment. But for me, I hadn't even

---

[4] https://infogalactic.com/info/Mourning

processed my loss yet, I had to make a decision about the burial, and it took place on the same day, for reasons that were unknown to me. No one asked us, the kids, about the date, and I don't think any of us had any knowledge of what was the appropriate time or day to bury your mother. But I would have liked for her to stay at least a day or two, so I could try and wrap my head around the loss I was experiencing.

Weirdly, once again, I was in the spotlight. Everyone wanted to know what my plans were. Was I getting married? Having children? Finished traveling? But the questions didn't end there. Most of my family felt they should intervene on behalf of my dead mother by saying how it was my mom's wish for me to get married and have kids. I didn't know if my other sisters got it as bad as I did, but for me it was particularly brutal given the breakup with Brian that no one knew about. I sat there day in and day out feeling unworthy, ashamed, vulnerable, and clueless, until I suddenly believed everyone's words and blamed myself for my mother's unhappy life. I questioned my relationship with the universe and life in general. Because if I was supposed to follow my heart, be honest and responsible to my own truth, how could I be doing so much damage to the people I loved, especially my mother?

I didn't know if I could sink any lower; I was fading by the minute. There was no time to mourn my mother. I was haunted by the questions and surrounded by people who expected answers. My mother was not there to defend me, and I was too exhausted to fight, argue, and justify my life as I did before. And at that point, I didn't even think my life was worth fighting for. *If all these people can tell me how wrong and sad my life has been,* I thought, *then they must be right.* I kept going deeper and deeper into that cold, dark place.

In the following days, I decided to acknowledge my loss the only way I knew. I wrote an email to my friends around the world. I also decided to apply for the new passport at the

Abyssinian Nomad

Canadian Embassy in Addis that I had told my mother about. The process would take a minimum of three weeks.

My father appeared to age in those few weeks more than he had in the last ten years. I was both saddened and scared for him. I thought I needed to be very careful around him. The last thing I wanted was to make him worry about me, so I tiptoed in my father's house and around Addis until my passport arrived. My confidence was gone. I felt ashamed that all my mother's friends and family thought I was a total loser (though they were kind enough not to use a word like that), and I didn't know what to do next.

In the meantime, I met Jules, a Quebecois man, who happened to be at the embassy at the same time as I was. He was getting a new passport, trying to work on a Nile basin initiative in East Africa. My passport still had two years left before it expired, but it had run out of pages.

Jules and I quickly became friends. I was relieved to find someone who could make me feel normal again rather than guilty about my life. We started seeing each other often; we'd meet in cafes and sat and talked for hours because there wasn't much else to do. I told him about what was going on in my life, my losses (my mother and Brian) and my dreams of traveling. He shared stories of his breakup, his future plans in Africa, and his wishes.

It was clear we were both looking to be rescued in some way. I couldn't say much about him, but I sensed he just wanted to get married and check that off his list as soon as possible. He seemed to realize that he was getting older. And as for me, I was in hell. I had wondered what the priest was talking about when he described hell as a place we go after we die. I always said my heaven and hell were on Earth. And at that moment, I felt I was right inside hell.

When Jules suddenly showed up in my life, and I found out he was interested in me, I thought it was divine intervention, giving me a chance to make things right. So, I decided to please my dead mother and maybe other people along the way, like all the family and friends who said they would pray for me. Yes, I wanted to make them happy and give them a break from worrying about me, and most of all set them free.

The relationship accelerated so fast I don't remember what happened when. We both wanted it so badly, I don't think either of us was thinking straight. The age difference was noticeable, maybe Jules looked a lot older than his age, but I didn't care. The very same friends who'd told me my life was doomed were now pointing out the age difference. I was confused! I thought they wanted me to find someone and settle down and that age was not a problem. I was an emotional wreck.

The next few weeks passed fast. My father was happy I had stayed around, and he seemed to like Jules, though he also seemed very confused about what was going on. He didn't know what had happened to Brian—I only told my sisters about Brian much later. Once our passports arrived, I had slowly started to reveal that I would like to finish my Cape to Cairo journey. I got a mixed reaction, but I wasn't asking for permission. I thought if I had come that far to make everyone happy, then I deserved to fulfill my dream too.

Jules and I sat and talked for hours about how to make things work. I even took a side trip with him to Khartoum in Sudan to support his bid for a project on the Nile river. There was one big issue where Jules and I didn't see eye to eye. He was friendly, but trusting people wasn't his strongest point. He was okay with my solo traveling, but while he didn't openly oppose couchsurfing and staying with strangers, he didn't like the idea at all. He also wanted to know my plans and what would happen once I got to Cairo. Where did I plan to settle? When did I want to get married? My answer was simply that I didn't know. From the outside, it looked like I was perfectly well and functioning, but something had died within me. All I wanted to do was go and be on the road once again. That was the only thing that felt right. Anything else I said or did seemed wrong.

Chapter 18: Emerging from the Ashes

"Rwanda is one of the smallest nations in the world. It is roughly the size of Vermont. The big difference is that Vermont has a population of about 600,000 whereas Rwanda has a population of 10 million making it one of the most densely populated countries in the world."
~ Rwanda 5 fun facts

"MY MOTHER IS DEAD. My mother is dead. My mother is dead!" I told myself again and again, as if by saying those words I would accept the truth about my mother's death and give myself permission to move forward. I was finally on the road again, but nothing felt the same in me. Things had changed in my life. I had changed. There was no boyfriend to accompany me on my journey—Jules was in Asia, and we were planning to meet back in Ethiopia later—nor was there a mother to call to share my excitement of crossing borders. No one would carefully follow my travels. Yes, I had friends around the world who expected the mass emails I sent whenever I got the inspiration, time, and of course, internet that worked. Still, I felt alone in a way I had never felt before in my life.

"This is it," I told myself. "This is my new life, and it all begins now." I was checking in my backpack on the Ethiopian Airlines flight to Kigali, Rwanda. My father had insisted on dropping me off at the airport, but I refused to let him come inside the terminal, saying it would be crowded. The truth was I just couldn't handle saying goodbye to him; a quick kiss in the car and running with my backpack felt much more doable.

The airport felt like a very safe and familiar place. I didn't look back to the entrance of the airport after checking in, just walked straight to immigration to get my passport stamped and go inside the departure lounge.

I decided I'd have to sleep or pretend to sleep on the plane so no one would talk to me. I was just worried about what I might say.

Hi, my name is Maski, and my mother is dead! —It was all I could think.

~~~

In 1994 as the Rwandan genocide was taking place, I remember watching BBC News, feeling my heart crush for the first time as an adult, and questioning our humanity in general.

I grew up listening to the one-channel TV and radio we had in Ethiopia; they talked about war and poverty most of the time. Ethiopia had been in the middle of a thirty-year civil war, and the news was all about it. But I was very young and didn't feel the helplessness and hopelessness I had as I watched the news on Rwanda. I was also confused and saddened by how the entire world watched and did nothing as the tragedy unfolded.

I wondered what happened to "We Are the World, We Are the Children," the song that had inspired me and made me feel one with the world. With that feeling rooted in my core, all I could think was that my generation had failed. But at the same time, a seed of desire had been planted in my heart that someday I would visit Rwanda.

~~~

Still, when I found myself in the capital city, Kigali, I wondered if Rwanda was a good place to continue my travels. It was the worst time of my life. I was emotionally bankrupt and weak. But Rwanda was the next country on my path crossing Africa overland, so I thought maybe it was a sign: the country had gone through so much and survived it. It was a symbol of human strength. Did it mean that I, too, would survive my loss and maybe find peace within? Knowing deep inside that our losses were incomparable, I asked myself whether Rwanda and Rwandan people could teach me how to cope.

I came out of the airport and breathed in the cool, fresh air. It wasn't the hot, humid air that had welcomed me in most parts of East Africa. I threw my backpack in the back seat of the taxi and jumped in the passenger side, giving the driver my couchsurfing host's address. The taxi driver marveled at how alike Rwandans and Ethiopians look; I had heard that we share the same ancestors.

I was busy breathing in the fresh air when suddenly my eyes filled with tears. They poured out in every direction before I could hide them. Though it worried the taxi driver, who barely spoke English, I knew what those tears meant. They meant: I was free to do what I wanted, I was alone, I was happy to be back on the road again. And the tears also meant I could finally mourn my mother without anyone telling me how to do it "properly," interrupting with words like "Menuew zeme alshie?" (Why are you quiet?)

What I didn't know at the time was that I couldn't schedule my appointments with grief, that it could strike anytime, anywhere, and it could express itself in many ways that I couldn't have imagined. I was never ready for my mother's death, and I didn't think I would have been ready even if I'd had a hundred years to prepare. But it had happened, and I felt like I was on a roller-coaster ride every day.

I fell in love, looking at the hills that surrounded Kigali. No wonder Kigali is known as the "City of a Thousand Hills." It was like no other African city I had been to: there was order; it was calm, and it was clean. I like order and systems that work in cities. When I arrived at my host's place, my room was waiting for me.

For the last three months in Ethiopia, the bathroom floors had been my only escape where I sat or stood under the cold shower (when there was running water) for a little privacy. Having personal space was almost unheard of in Ethiopia and never encouraged, especially at the time of a loss of a loved one. Now I had a room and I was happy; the small things that we take for granted usually surprise us in different ways.

My host was a Belgian single working mother with an adorable boy, who gave me great tips on where to start, what to see, and where to go. She offered me her place as my base to return to as I explored the country.

One of my favorite things to do when I travel to a new country is to read books written by local writers (not the guidebooks written by other tourists and travelers). But I felt like I had already done my homework. Though this one wasn't by a local writer, I had already read books like *Shake Hands with the Devil*, by a Canadian, Lt. Gen. Roméo Dallaire, who witnessed atrocities while leading a UN peacekeeping mission to Rwanda. I had also read *Left to Tell*, which is the incredible true story of survival, faith, and ultimately forgiveness.

Maskarm Haile

Twenty-two-year-old Immaculee Ilibagiza survived the Rwandan genocide by hiding with seven other starving women in a tiny bathroom for ninety-one terrifying days.

Then there was *Hotel Rwanda*, about a Hutu man, Paul Rusesabagina, played by Don Cheadle, who managed the Hotel des Mille Collines and lived a happy life with his Tutsi wife, played by Sophie Okonedo, and their three children. Paul Rusesabagina took in Tutsis fleeing the killings at the height of the Rwandan genocide. I had tears flowing down my face years ago, in 2005, when I watched the movie in Vancouver with an audience at the University of British Columbia. After the film had ended, there was a question and answer period. Shakily, I raised my hand and asked, "Why did the world stay silent while all those people died? Why didn't you do anything?"

My suppressed anger had surfaced once again, many years later. I was certain it was the first time I'd put my hand up with so much emotion and anger. In my despair, I had completely forgotten the difference between a movie crew and the UN employees.

My first day in Kigali was very hard. I decided to visit the Kigali Genocide Memorial, where hundreds of thousands of people — men, women, and children — are buried. Once again, I felt sick to my stomach. How could we fail so much as human beings?

The next day, I took the early morning bus to Kibuye; it was about a three-hour ride to the lakeside town. Kibuye is a small town situated on the hills above the long and beautiful lake, offers a great view of the turquoise-hued water and scattered islands. Only two things occupied my mind in my three-hour bus ride on the twisting and turning road in the hills. I thought of my mother. I wondered what she would have said and thought of my traveling after her death. Would she have been happy for me, would she have worried, or

Abyssinian Nomad

would she have been angry with me for continuing with my journey? The other thing that occupied my mind was how a beautiful place like Rwanda, so abundant in nature, could have gone through such horror.

I met up with a local couchsurfer, Patrick, for coffee and a bit of sightseeing. He offered to walk with me and show me around where his family used to live and the church used to be. Everything he was talking about seemed to be in the past, so I was afraid to ask questions, worried it might upset him.

Patrick was a tall and soft-spoken young man who didn't say much unless he had a question to ask. I got us soft drinks from the hotel, and we sat by the water to chat and get to know each other before we embarked on a village tour.

I was reading my guidebook while I waited for him, so he was fascinated by how seriously I was taking my trip. He asked why I came from Ethiopia if I was going from south to north. To which I told him how I recently lost my mother, with tears in my eyes. He looked at me for a while, sadness in his eyes, and said, "I am sorry!"

I followed up with a question about his family. Patrick said he didn't know exactly how old he is: he was very young when his father asked his brother and him to run into the bush and hide during the genocide. While in the forest he got separated from his brother. He said, slowly and consciously, that he is the only survivor in his family. It sounded more like a question than a statement.

But then, looking at me at a loss for words, he quickly said that was a long time ago. Things had changed a lot since then, and he was living a devoted Christian life serving others. And that broke my heart. I will never know his loss or be able to say I understand what he has been through.

The next day, while having breakfast in my hotel, I met another Belgian expat. We chatted a bit over breakfast and he told me his plan to go to Napoleon Island on Lake Kivu with his friends for the day and invited me to join them if I would like.

As it was also on my to-do list, I was grateful for the opportunity to share the cost of the boat and have people to hang out with. They were all expats; I was the only traveler. We swapped travel stories, swam in the lake, and picnicked, all of us happy to be in nature. It was a different vibe than I'd experienced the previous day. Each time I took a deep dive into the lake, I felt the water cleansing me, taking away the heaviness in my body and my mind. I slowly started to feel that I was breathing once again.

The day I left Kigali, I was standing in the middle of a vibrant open market in the early morning, waiting to catch a bus to Gisenyi. Suddenly a bunch of young men wearing pink shorts and shirts, surrounded by three policemen, walked past me. The market went quiet. I wondered what had happened. I noticed that people were avoiding eye contact and not looking at the men. Many stopped what they were doing and just waited for them to pass. I was standing alone, I had no idea what was going on, but I could feel the heaviness in the air. Once we were on the bus, I found out those men were prisoners going to court for their hearing. The man next to me said, "It was those kids that killed many people." They must have been very young when the genocide happened, because they still looked very young. And those men were paraded in the market in front of the people, who had lost their families and friends, because the court was in town.

Witnessing that scene overwhelmed me, but at the same time, I learned a significant lesson in compassion, forgiveness, letting go, and the need to move on, something that would help me in my journey later.

~~~

Abyssinian Nomad

Most people I talked to suggested it wasn't safe for me to cross the border into the Democratic Republic of Congo (DRC). I loved Congolese music and the intense energy that emanated from most Congolese. I was hoping to experience some Congolese culture, food, and music, and, if I could, I wanted to climb the active volcano that had erupted in 2002.

But the news coming out of Brazzaville and the DRC wasn't very encouraging. And I didn't know anyone currently living there who could give me information. I slowly withdrew the idea and packed a small backpack, leaving most of my things, including my yellow fever card and the copy of my big Lonely Planet Guide to Africa, at my host's place in Kigali, and took the bus to Gisenyi, Rwanda.

The bus ride took seven hours, and all my thoughts were fixated on the DRC. The DRC had been at war for years before it made another headline when in 2002, Mount Nyiragongo erupted and killed many people and left over 200,000 homeless.

Once I arrived there, I instantly liked Gisenyi. I found the guesthouse that was recommended by numerous travelers, checked myself in, and went out to explore the town. I wandered around visiting the market; my smiles were quickly met with wonder from the locals, as I looked very much like them. They seemed to be questioning why I was greeting them.

I slowly made my way to the famous sandy beach, Tam Tam Bikini, for the sunset, a perfect place for a little contemplation. I was within walking distance of the DRC border. Some locals were setting up their BBQ and drinks stalls, getting ready for the locals who would be coming after work.

I decided to sit in one of the empty plastic chairs and ordered myself a Sprite, watching the sunset, and feeling angry about not being able to go to the DRC, Somalia, or Eritrea. All because of war.

Maskarm Haile

As the sunset's beautiful colors momentarily took over the sky, my negative emotions faded, and I found myself in a state of bliss. One of the beautiful things that Brian and I used to do (and I continue to do) was to watch the sunrise and sunset whenever we got a chance. I loved how it unwound me and grounded my experience for the day by allowing me to reflect. It was the time when I was the most filled with gratitude, rather than wanting to see or do more.

At that very moment, I reminded myself how far I had come in my journey and that I still had a lot to discover and experience. I had so much to be grateful for, including that I was back on the road. As that thought ran through my mind, I saw a young white guy approaching my table. He said that the previous week he had sat in the same spot watching the sunset and asked if he could join me. "Sure," I said, thinking, *Great, another tourist. But wait,* I thought, *he said last week.* He spent a week in Gisenyi. *What was he doing?* I decided that he must have been an expat working there. All that was going through my head until he came back with drinks he'd bought from the boys selling them on the beach.

We quickly introduced ourselves; it is unbelievable how traveling turns everyone into a long-lost brother or sister in a matter of seconds. We could trust each other, or at the very least give each other the benefit of the doubt. I found out my new companion, Fabian, was a German traveler who'd managed to cross the border into the DRC. I interrogated him for most of the evening. By the time we said goodbye after a long walk and dinner, I had decided to cross the border the next morning. He gave me his guidebook and DRC SIM card for my phone, which I promised to give back to him in a few days.

But the question was, who should I call if anything happened? No one knew or would understand why I was there in the first place. Not even my new boyfriend, who was in Asia

Abyssinian Nomad

at that point, would understand why I was going to the DRC. I decided to send a quick email to Brian, so that someone at least knew where I was.

Fabian walked me a little way back to my guesthouse and wished me luck. Armed with a guidebook and a new sense of adventure, I walked to my guesthouse, but there was one little problem: I had booked my room for three days, and it was only my first night. When I walked in, there was a little elderly lady sitting behind the table. Someone else had checked me in. I wondered if she was the owner. There were a few men around, some watching TV and one reading. I slowly scanned the room and walked to the table, feeling guilty for what I was about to do—cancel my booking.

The woman was cheerful and curious about me. Apparently, she had heard a bit about me from the other women, but she hadn't believed I was traveling Africa as a solo African woman. I jumped at the opportunity to tell her I wanted to cross the border to the DRC in the morning and cancel two nights of my booking. The woman stopped smiling and looked at me seriously. Feeling guilty, I decided I would just pay the money and go if it was going to be a big problem.

But I quickly learned that the booking wasn't the problem. The elderly woman kept saying that I was the problem! She got louder and louder, and everyone could hear now. Some of the guests turning around to look at us. When a man who was reading a book, looked up, our eyes met, and I saw the title of the book he was reading, (I always love checking out the title of the books people read, it's as if it tells me something about them.) I got a glimpse of the title, *L'Abyssinie*, a historical novel which was written in French by Jean-Christohe. I had read long ago translated into English. The story was set in 1700, towards the end of the region of Louis XIV; it follows the fortunes of a brave apothecary, a talented but unofficial doctor, who is talked into leading an embassy from Cairo to Ethiopia.

Maskarm Haile

It was as if we were connected by that magical book he was holding—his first word was "Èthiopie?" All I could say was "oui"

It was in that moment, I heard my inner voice say, Abyssinian Nomad. I smile. He said, "Bienvenue au Rwanda," with a heart-warming smile!

I had never seen him before, but something sparked between us and I instantly felt safe around him.

The woman didn't waste time. She told him how I was traveling alone and I wanted to cross the border the next day. Only then did I understand why she kept saying I was a problem. She didn't like the idea, and she wanted that man to tell me how dangerous it would be for me. She promised to take care of me and to organize some trips for me if I would stay. It felt like a mother pleading with her daughter. It was hard to see her being so emotional about someone she had only just met.

I introduced myself to my new friend Kevin and explained what I was doing in Gisenyi. It was evident that we had bonded over that ancient book that talked about Ethiopian history in great length. I mentioned that I wanted to go to the DRC the next day. Little did I know, Kevin was a tour guide from the DRC, who drove for well-heeled tourists who stayed at a luxury hotel, and he was spending the night at the guesthouse. *How is that for a sign?* I thought?

Since he was a regular in the guesthouse, the owner knew him, and that was why she was looking to have him talk me out of going to the DRC. But instead, he was fascinated by the Abyssinian nomad he had just met, and he wanted to do everything possible to make my dream come true. He said his guests were older people who usually only needed him after ten thirty in the morning. If I was willing to wake up early and pay for his car pass, he would drive me to the border and leave me somewhere safe in the town of Goma. I almost jumped up and down. The woman wasn't impressed, but she was happy, at least. She trusted him.

I couldn't believe my luck! The level of universe intervention in one day was heartwarming. I barely slept that night. I sent a quick email to Brian with my DRC telephone number, just in case. I was happy; at least one person knew where I was heading.

Chapter 19: But You Are Black

"The Democratic Republic of the Congo is the second largest country in Africa. It borders nine countries: Angola, Burundi, the Central African Republic, the Republic of Congo, Rwanda, South Sudan, Tanzania, Uganda, and Zambia."
~ 11 facts about DRC

I MET KEVIN AT BREAKFAST but was so excited I could barely eat anything. I put my small bag in his car, and we started driving. I could hardly believe I was actually on my way to the DRC. The drive was breathtaking, but more than that, I was touched by the kindness of humanity. Everyone I met seemed to want help me accomplish my dream.

At the border, there was lots of confusion. It was the most awkward border crossing I had ever experienced. I was sent from one official to another, from one room to another, as the immigration officers tried to figure out what I was doing.

Border officer: "Is your family in Goma?"

I assumed that he thought my parents must work for the UN.

Me: "No."

Officer: "Ah... Your husband works for the UN?"
Me: "No."
Officer: "No? Why are you here then?"
Me: "I need a tourist visa, please!"
Officer: "Tourist? But you're black!"

They all stopped what they were doing and looked at me. There were four officers in that tiny room, but none of them said a word. They just stared at me. I was still standing with my passport, form, and money in my hand.

Because I had been gone for a while, Kevin came inside the office looking for me, wondering why it was taking me long. He explained to them how I had been traveling in Africa for months now. My husband was in Canada (my imaginary husband!), and Kevin was going to drop me off in the city and then come back.

The decision by the guards was a unanimous, "No!"

They all spoke at the same time. They all said the same thing: that it was dangerous for me to go anywhere alone.

I stood there, tears in my eyes, like a kid, when Kevin intervened once again on my behalf. Some of them knew him because he crossed the border often with tourists. He said that he was taking responsibility for me. He gave them his telephone number, name, address, and a possible hotel where I might be staying.

As one of the officers took my passport and the US $35 for the visa, another officer asked for my yellow fever card.

My heart sank.

My card was in Kigali. Once again there was a huge commotion. "You are Canadian," one of the officers shouted, as if Canadians needed the card more than anyone else.

Another immigration officer took Kevin outside to talk to him. I knew they wanted money now and I was getting irritated. I refused to acknowledge what they were saying. I argued that I had been vaccinated for yellow fever and that I wouldn't travel around Africa without one—I cared about my health. Apparently, Kevin paid them off. He wouldn't tell me how much or take any money from me, though; when I asked, he just laughed. And his time was running out—he wanted to get me into the city before his guests called for him.

Unfortunately, the immigration officers still insisted that I could not leave the town of Goma. Apparently, I needed a permit to leave each town because I would be stopped at the checkpoints. Right there, my dream of seeing the active volcano died. But I told myself at least I would be in Goma.

The first thing I noticed crossing the border was the number of UN cars zooming past us on that dangerous road. The way they were driving was insane. But I quickly realized that was the normal way of driving in the DRC. I had been on lots of bad roads, but nothing compared to those. And, of course, I heard Congolese music everywhere. The sound was coming from the small shops in town.

In the distance, I could see small planes landing and taking off. With the UN peacekeepers driving around and the dust blowing, it was like a scene from a movie.

Kevin's guests called to let him know they would soon be ready to be picked up from their hotel. We were already in town, and he had taken me to see the lava that damaged the town when the volcano erupted. But he still wanted to make sure I found a place to stay before he left me. Only a few hotels were considered safe by the UN, and they were not budget friendly, but since my safety was at stake, I was willing to pay way more than usual. Kevin was relieved to find a safe place for me to stay; we exchanged contact numbers, and he set off, back to Gisenyi to meet up with his guests. We never got another chance to see each other, as he was in Rwanda when I got back, but I was grateful to both him and Fabian. Of course, Brian called as soon as he got my email.

Abyssinian Nomad

When I got to my room, I discovered I had a beautiful view of the lake. I could see Rwanda in the distance and the wild and lush green forest of the DRC. It was another moment of bliss. I sat on the balcony of my deluxe room, thinking about how much had happened since last night, and drinking Sprite—*a little celebration before I hit the town,* I thought.

It was evident there wasn't much to see or do in the city, and I only had a permit to stay in town. But I didn't let that get me down. I could always meet people and do things with locals. And, who knew, maybe I could even sneak into the small towns! I was ready for a new adventure, but there was one problem. The hotel where I was staying was safe because of all the security, and it was too far outside of the town to be within walking distance of anything, and there were no taxis in sight.

The reception staff didn't think I was there alone when I checked in. Later, the staff told me they were sure my family or husband would join me—but when they learned about my plans, they looked horrified. One of the Indian men kept saying, "No! No, no!" as if I hadn't heard his first "No!" when I asked about going out on my own. And to call a taxi would take at least an hour, he said.

Oh well. I needed to come up with some way to leave the hotel. I took the address, and the phone number for the manager, and went out for a walk while they all stood looking at me in horror. At the gate, the security officers called the hotel reception desk to confirm that I could leave the hotel compound. As I was walking through the gate, a man on a bike was also going through the gate. Thinking that he was a hotel employee, I signaled for him to stop. He didn't speak very much English, but he was polite, and as perplexed as anyone could be in those circumstances.

I politely introduced myself, and I asked if he could give me a ride to town. He simply said, "Town?" He didn't seem to fully understand what I was saying, but he told me to sit on his bike. He took me to town, braking every so often to turn and look at me. At times, he slowed down to ask if I knew what I was doing. I showed him the name of the places I wanted to see—the church and the market—and asked if he knew any taxi drivers or tour companies. He did not.

When I asked him what the hotel guests came to see in Goma, he was even more perplexed. It turned out he didn't work for the hotel; he was there for a meeting. Embarrassed, I apologized.

He was quick to mention that as a woman I should never ask a stranger for a ride again. Ever! "*Jamais, jamais, jamais!*" he said, using both his minimal English and French with a very firm and almost angry tone. *Oh, my! Thank God I am not your sister or wife,* I said in my heart. And also thinking, *how dangerous is this place?*

In town, more shops were open, and music blared from the speakers. He stopped his bike and gave me an instruction—more like an order. He pointed to an internet cafe across the street. He told me to go there and to wait for him. He said I could use the internet if I wanted but that I didn't have to because the owners were his friends and they would let me stay. He had to do something and would return in thirty minutes to take me to the places I want to go. And in return, I could pay for his gas, if I wanted. Then he disappeared. I didn't know his name or have his number. Was I supposed to sit and wait for thirty minutes? And would that be thirty minutes in African time? It was the one thing that killed me over and over: the relationship people have with time in Africa. People were even late for weddings. And now I was supposed to trust some random guy in Goma?

But I decided to give him the benefit of the doubt.

His friend at the internet cafe was friendly; we tried to have a conversation in my broken French, and I used the internet to pass time and answered my couchsurfing emails. But before I knew it, my new friend was back, standing there and smiling at me. I introduced myself to him formally, and he said his name was Yves. He told his cafe friends how he met me, and everyone in the cafe marveled at my courage, but they all said the same thing: "*Jamais, jamais, jamais* hitchhike." They could see that I didn't accept what they were saying, and one of them said only hookers do that in Africa and that no decent woman in her right mind would stand on the street to ask for a ride.

In my desperation to show that I was not crazy, I showed the couchsurfing website to Yves so he could see that there are thousands of people around the world who do what I was doing, and also how many are like him, who generously do what he was doing for me. He seemed a little bit interested but didn't say much.

And then we were on the bike once again.

He showed me around. He was one of the earthly angels that graced my life. Things would have been so hard and maybe even dangerous if I'd been walking around on my own. Although he couldn't sneak me into the nearby Pigmy village, because of the checkpoints, I got to hangout in a local bar where the Congolese music blared out of a huge speaker and people danced after drinking a few beers. The time wasn't right to visit the DRC, I admit, but I am so grateful for being able to see as much as I did, and for the connection I made with the locals.

The next day, Yves asked me how he could become a couchsurfer. I was pleased to create the very first couchsurfer profile in Goma for him before leaving town!

Fabian and I met up in Gisenyi and decided to travel to Kigali together. He had booked a guesthouse not far from where I was couchsurfing, and we had dinner and watched a traditional dance at the famous Hôtel des Mille Collines which is featured the movie *Hotel Rwanda*, and which, after years of renovation, had reopened to the public.

Fabian had one more thing to check off on his Africa bucket list before leaving East Africa and I, too, had the same wish on my list: white-water rafting on the source of the Nile, in Jinja, Uganda. I couldn't be happier. I had found a partner in crime.

Chapter 20: Are You One of Us?

"Uganda is truly the pearl of Africa."
~ *Winston Churchill*

THAT NIGHT, SITTING IN MY room at my couchsurfing home, I sat and cried uncontrollably. I missed my mother deeply. I'd had a strong urge to call her many times on this trip, wishing to hear her voice, to tell her about my travels, forgetting I couldn't do that anymore. I was told by my spiritual teachers and read in numerous books that though she would be gone physically, she will always be with me in spirit. I believed that before her death, and I desperately wanted to believe it. But, now that she was gone, I struggled to accept it. I just wanted my mother. Not her spirit, *her* in her body and mind. Finally, I cried myself to sleep.

The next morning, Fabian and I took the long bus ride to Kampala. At the border, we stood to pay for our visa and get our stamp. The immigration officer, to whom I was about to hand my passport and the $50 for my visa, stared at me a bit.

Looking proud for identifying my features, he said: "You Ethiopian?"

Me: "Yes." I hoped he wouldn't be unhappy with me when I took out my passport.

Officer: "Where are you going?"

Me: "Kampala first and Jinja, and then I plan to travel around Uganda."

Officer: "Why?"

Me: "Because I like traveling."

Officer: "Black tourist?"

Me: "Kind of." I didn't know what else to say. This wasn't the first time I'd heard that.

Now another officer joined the conversation and asked: "Do you have family?"

I almost wanted to say No and tell them how I lost my mother but I said, "Yes, they are in Ethiopia." I didn't want to go into detail about losing my mother.

Officer: "Are you married? You have kids?"

Me: "No, but, but ... my husband is in Canada."

The officer cursed my imaginary husband, saying he wasn't a man for letting me wander around Africa on my own.

Officer: "No problem, I will marry you!! You know, a woman shouldn't be going around alone like that. It's a shame for an African family."

I didn't have anything to say to that, but I was so glad none of my family were there, as I was sure my mother had feared people would think I didn't have a family, and now her worst fear had come true.

It seemed that Fabian and I were the only tourists on the bus. The other passengers just showed their passports or identity documents and passed through. Seeing the bus was waiting just for me, the officer stamped my passport.

I remember growing up hearing about Idi Amin, and how Uganda had been the pearl of Africa. My first contact with Ugandans were family friends who had lived in Addis Ababa for a few years. They had young children, and I remembered how well the girls could dance. The other thing I admired and loved about them was that they were free to talk and express themselves in a way I would never be able to do. Most Ethiopians were raised to be very self-conscious, to the extent of not looking the elders in the eye and never talking around adults. What a contrast that was!

As an adult, the thing most people mentioned about Kampala was the nightlife hub. My plan was simple when I reached Uganda: I would go white-water rafting, experience the nightlife, and track gorillas. My original plan included spending a few weeks in western Uganda as a volunteer in a community school in a small village. I had found a couchsurfer who was running a community school, and he offered to host me. He was asking couchsurfers to spend some time with him and his family to experience local culture while making a difference, and I had thought that was a brilliant idea.

I had been exchanging emails with him, but now things had changed. I was supposed to go back to Ethiopia to meet up with Jules, and I was starting to dread it. I felt the relationship was stopping me from taking my time and being able to go with the flow. So far, all of Jules's emails were asking me when I was coming back to Ethiopia. And he was already mad at me for not knowing the exact day.

In the last few years of my travels, I had skydived, bungee jumped, parachuted, paraglided, and dived the Great Barrier Reef, but none of that had prepared me for white-water rafting on the Nile. It was by far one of the hardest things I had ever done in my life. I am not a strong swimmer, but I love the water. I had never been in a river that shook me from side to side, and up and down in a such an intense way. Only later, when I watched the video, did I realize that most of the time it was the river guides who were flipping the raft for fun, not that the wild water was capsizing the raft. It may have seemed impressive for the spectators, but I was terrified.

Maskarm Haile

White-water rafting was life-changing for me, because it was about surrendering. The first thing, or maybe the only thing, I heard on the safety briefing was, "In the event of the raft capsizing, you don't need to hang on to the handle. There is no use in fighting because you may break your bones or lose your hand." The first time I heard that I thought, *What a contrast*. It went against all I knew, but later on it made sense. We tend to hold onto things rather than let go.

My life at the time felt like I was going through rapids, and all I could try to do was stay above the water and breathe. Yes, there were times when I went under and came back up again, and that was okay. The trick was to stay on top and not sink to the bottom, while at the same time examining my thoughts, finding out what I was holding on to (ideas, belief systems, relationships, etc.), and letting it all go. My simple goal and mantra for my four-hour rafting trip was to stay above the water! Stay above the water! Stay above the water!

The Ethiopians have such an attachment to the Nile River, and growing up in Ethiopia meant that I too had an attachment to water. I was also lucky enough to have seen the Blue Nile waterfall in Ethiopia; I walked miles to get there, just to feel the sprinkle of the water touching my face. I was mesmerized by it, but that had been a long time ago. At the source of the Nile in Uganda, the water looked murky, still, and infinite. It was both inviting and foolishly deceiving for anyone who thought that mighty river was calm. There was something about the majestic river that touched my spirit just by looking at it. Maybe it was because I knew how rich in history that river was, how abundant it was, and how it was the lifeline for East and North Africa.

After adjusting our life vest and helmets, it was too late to back out. Where we started, the water seemed calm as we rowed in unison and chatted, getting to know our excited group from around the world and the local river guides. Being the only black women on the boat made me feel maybe there is a reason why other Africans don't do this. But there was no time to worry about that now: very soon we started hearing and seeing the raging and beautifully white grade one rapid, that was mentioned again and again as being easy. But we capsized. Or should I say, the guide thought it was fun idea and flipped the raft and we were thrown into the unforgiving current. It was exhilarating!

After a few more grade three and four rapids, the river guide called out, "The Bad Place!" ... Yes, the rapids in Jinja were really named "The Bad Place." "The Bad Place" *was* really bad, and I must have misheard that it was the last one. The rapids all seemed and felt the same unforgiven to me. By the time we got to the penultimate one, I saw some people leaving the boat, but it didn't even occur to me I should be doing the same. I had already been repeatedly beneath the water, tossed around, and I didn't think leaving the boat was what I should do.

Big mistake! All I remember was being tossed out high into the air and landing in the white water that roared ferociously while I screamed for my life. It was cold and dark, and I was bumping into the vicious rocks underwater, praying that I didn't break any bones.

Suddenly, I heard someone saying, "Don't fight the water." Who said that? Was it the river guide from earlier that morning, or someone else? But all I wanted to say was, *"Can't you see, I'm dying?"* Something shot me up to the surface and at that very moment, in a split second, I locked eyes with one of the kayakers. I thought one of the gods of the river was coming to save me. While he was dragging me out of danger, all I could think was how funny it was that we had willingly paid our money and signed consent forms to give away our lives.

I was lucky to survive with a little bit of bruising on my arms and legs, and as much as I loved my experience and would never trade it for anything else in the world, I told myself it would be a long time before I'd go white-water rafting again.

We got back to Kampala for a night before I said goodbye to Fabian as he was flying out and I headed to western Uganda. Though my plan to volunteer didn't materialize, I got an invitation from Mukasa, and his family, to host me for few days in a community in the small village on Lake Lyantonde.

I took a six-hour bus ride, plus a two-hour cramped communal taxi ride, on a bumpy road. But it was worth every minute of it. I instantly fell in love with Uganda's beauty. The surroundings in Uganda were a dark green, and the fruits and vegetables looked so vibrant and fresh.

My host, Mukasa, and his family welcomed me graciously. My tiny room didn't have electricity or water but had the most breathtaking view of a crater lake surrounded by green hills. I was invited for dinner at my host's residence along with another couchsurfer from Australia who was volunteering in the village.

Dinner was as exotic as it could get: we ate a delicacy of white ant with "pasho," a dish made of maize flour or sorghum, and plantain. I'd made an agreement with the universe a long time ago. I think deep inside at a soul level, I knew that maybe one day I would be traveling the world. But I wanted to be a gracious guest, so I made a promise to eat whatever people cooked for me. When I was growing up, my grandmother didn't allow me to eat food at other people's houses, especially if they were Muslim. The same went for the Muslim families; my friends weren't allowed to eat in our home. It wasn't that we obeyed the rules, of course. My friends ate in our house, and we ate in theirs, and everyone kept it secret. But the truth was, I was tired of that. It didn't make sense to me, so I promised if ever I got the chance to travel, I would eat anything. I mean anything, because as an Ethiopian growing up, there were so many things we refrained from eating. So now I had been eating lobsters, mussels, squid, crocodile, frogs, kudos, camel...

That day in Mukasa's house, with only two lamps on the small table and barely enough light to see, I could hardly make out what I was eating. But I was determined to keep my promise. The Australian woman, Allison, and I looked at each other as if we were encouraging each other. We put a little serving of the ants on our plates. It tasted creamy and the texture was softer in my mouth than anything I'd tried before—but nevertheless, I was grateful to my hosts for preparing their delicacy in honor of us.

The next day, I went to visit the community school where Allison was teaching. I played with the children, and when she finished her work, we set out to explore the village. I was struck by the beautiful crater lakes that surrounded the village.

On the way back, we stopped by the plot right next to the community place where we were couchsurfing, and a young Mzungu (the locals call white people Mzungu), Lucas, came out to greet us. I could see a tent and some small shade, but nothing else on the land. He had a fire going. We sat around the fire, three wandering souls from three continents, sharing our stories about how we got there. The young man had bought the plot because he had fallen in love with the place, and he was living in his tent until he built a house on the land. Actually, he had an excellent idea about making a backpackers' paradise in the future. He was determined, and his willingness to endure everything else to make his dream come true was contagious.

That night and the next day, we explored each other's lives through our life stories. Both of them were younger than me and had come a long way from where they were born, and in life, to get to that village in Uganda. On the other hand, I was born almost right next door, but it had taken me lots of twists and turns to get to where I was. Being surrounded by the forests, with the dramatic backdrop of the crater lake, tropical birds, and friendly monkeys, I felt like it allowed me to unpack a little more of my life. It was as if mother nature had held me like a baby, and I was lying there feeling safe, and seeing things clearly once again.

I had been thinking about my mother and her dreams that would never come true, and my epic journey that had gotten me to this point in my life. I was more than halfway through my trip from Cape to Cairo, and it was both exciting and scary at the same time. Then, a little voice sneaked in and said, "What's next?" I felt a tightness my stomach, the kind I'd experienced when I was in Tanzania. Dizziness and lightheadedness all over again. I thought of Jules and his emails and texts. He was very impatient for me to get back, and he was also really concerned about me. Being in that beautiful place and sharing that conversation with those two strangers created a space within me where I felt there was more to my life than just pleasing my dead mother. It couldn't be my driving source for the rest of my life. Realizing and accepting that was a big relief and insight, but it didn't answer my question of what was next.

Lucas had to leave for Kampala the next day, and he called me later to tell me his friend was willing to host me and I could hang out with them in Kampala. I knew if I was going to experience nightlife in Kampala, I had to meet people who knew the place well and could host me to avoid traveling on my own at night. But in order to do that, I needed to get back to Kampala. To take the morning bus from Fort Portal, I had to set out on a crazy 30 km *boda-boda* (motorbike) ride, otherwise known as a silent killer by many, on a 30 km-long bumpy and dusty road, which turned my backpack and my body to a red murky color but got me to the bus just before it left to Kampala.

Abyssinian Nomad

Once again, I was back in the Nakasero open market in the heart of the Kampala bus stop, munching on avocado and grasshopper. There was congestion, craziness, and over-enthusiastic vendors who sold almost everything: food, to clothes, to car spare parts, and everything in between. Standing in the middle of it was as frightening as it was thrilling.

It was incredible how everything worked out for me. Adem was a young expat who had been living in Uganda for a while. His American roommate had just left for Europe, so I was given her room. He and Lucas introduced me to more of their friends, locals and expats, and Kampala became home for the next few days.

As crazy as it sounds, it was in the chaos of Kampala that I found its charm. English is widely spoken there, which made conversation a lot easier, and it was fun to randomly chitchat. Ugandans don't need much questioning to talk about life, safety and security, politics, religion, and corruption. They can find humor even in bad situations. Like most countries in Africa, everything started with greetings and questions like, *What is your religion? How old are you? Where is your family? Are you married?* Very personal, yet acceptable to ask.

I enjoyed my connections with locals and exploring Kampala's market, museums, cafes and neighbourhoods by day, and I hung out at night with my new friends and their friends, watching live music and bar hopping. My friends also decided to take me to the Ethiopian Village where they said we'd eat the best Ethiopian food in Kampala. I had heard there was a big Ethiopian and Eritrean community in Kampala.

While having lunch, we ended up talking about relationships, and I asked how it was for them being Mzungus and dating here. I had noticed the girls were a little aggressive, and walking into the bar and clubs at night with Lucas and

Adem had earned me a few looks. Lucas said it was hard being in the village, as he felt a little isolated. But Adem confirmed something my Montreal radar had suspected. He was gay! I was even more curious and asked what it was like to be gay in Africa. So far, it was only in South Africa where I met openly gay couples and individuals through couchsurfing. In some places, I avoided the topic because some people were still in denial about the existence of gay communities in Africa.

I was curious to know how much Uganda had embraced LGBTQ culture. It turned out while there was an enormous underground culture, the government was not so accepting.

Adem wanted to know if I would be going the underground gay club later that night with him. Of course I would be—I had even talked Lucas into coming along. I needed a partner in crime.

We took the *"boda-bodas"* (motorbikes) to the underground club. I was expecting a little bar, but it was a big club. And all the time, I was thinking, *It can't be just expats going there, so why is the topic still so sensitive?*

We were a little early, but the evening was lots of fun. I got to meet lots of Adem's friends. Lucas and I were probably the only newcomers, because most of the people seemed to know each other. I met men and women from Uganda, Rwanda, Burundi, Djibouti, and Congo. One of the Burundian men had a crush on Lucas and kept chasing him until I explained that Lucas was with me. But by then we were friends, so he said he was happy for me.

I had a deep, meaningful conversation with the three women Adem had introduced me to. These beautiful young ladies seemed confused about my relationship with Adem. I explained how I ended up at his house, and that very soon I would be on the road again.

Then I saw everyone become quiet... One of the brave ones among them, looking me in the eye, asked, "Are you one of us?"

Confused, I asked, "Do you mean African?" They all smiled... I got it. "No, no!" I said, feeling a little embarrassed for not understanding the first time.

Though they were puzzled about me showing up at a gay bar, they all seemed happy. One of them said her family and friends had never accepted her, so she was happy I was open-minded enough to come to the club to hang out. We all did a group hug and danced to that.

After the most unexpected, fun-filled, and insightful time in Uganda, it was time to say goodbye to my new friends once again, and to take the bus—this time to Nairobi, Kenya.

Chapter 21: The Man with an AK47 on the Bus

"Lake Nakuru, located in central Kenya, Nakuru is a shallow lake. It houses the world's greatest bird spectacle as millions of flamingos gather to feed on the abundant algae found on the lake."
~ Wikipedia

I TOOK A NIGHT BUS, so I arrived in Nairobi in the early morning. It was a dark, cold, rainy morning. The trip had started well, the roads were good, and the bus wasn't too full. Once again, I was probably the only one on the bus traveling with a passport since most of the passengers were locals or Kenyans traveling with their identity cards. As it got darker, the bus kept stopping a lot, and police kept jumping on and off checking our identity. They looked at me weirdly every time I gave them my passport. We also had to get off the bus for the bus to be searched. When I asked the man sitting next to me what was going on, he said he had overheard the police talking, and that particular night there was a group of people posing as police and robbing buses and individuals driving to Nairobi.

Abyssinian Nomad

At that moment, I wondered if taking a night bus was the wisest thing I could have done. I was on a bus in the middle of the night and had to worry about real and fake policemen. It was one of my longest nights, and I was relieved when I arrived safely in Nairobi at Kamau's apartment, my couchsurfing host.

Kenya is one of the East African countries I had already been to a few times before. It was where I experienced my first safari, and I had been to a few of the national parks over the years. On my big trip, I was planning to just pass through Kenya, but then I found out it was the season for the great migration.

Every year about two million animals cross Mara River from the Serengeti National Park in Tanzania to Masai Mara National Park in Kenya. I had watched it a few times on the National Geographic and Discovery Channels, and I wasn't going to miss it while in Kenya. It's one of the seven new wonders of the world.

In the meantime, I had been in touch with a Japanese traveler, Satomi, on a couchsurfing platform, with a possibility of traveling together to Ethiopia or even further. One of her friends Akio, from Tokyo, was joining her in Nairobi, and they planned to backpack all the way to Cairo. When we finally met, it was incredible how we clicked. We joked about Akio becoming our husband and protecting both of us.

We started by shopping around for the best deal that suited a backpacker budget and settled on a three-day safari to the Masai Mara National Park to see the migration and visit a Masai village.

It was a dark, cold, and rainy morning when we started driving to the Masai Mara National Park with a bunch of other tourists. The cheerful guide smilingly welcomed us onboard, while we all looked half-asleep, and regretted coming out of our warm beds. But all that changed the minute we entered the national park.

Maskarm Haile

To me, going on safari is like buying a lottery ticket. There are days we might miss the jackpot and come back tired, frustrated, and disappointed. And witnessing a migration is a double or triple jackpot because no one knows the exact date or time the crossing takes place. It's a season, and we've all seen the magic take place on the National Geographic Channel, but we never know how long the National Geographic photographer has had to sit and wait to take those pictures.

As the sun warmed up, so too did we become more alive and excited. We positioned ourselves so that we would be able to enjoy the best views. It felt like we'd hit the jackpot in the first hour, when we were lucky enough to see the hyenas running to find shelter as the day broke. We saw hippos, various types of deer, elephants, buffalos, and we even witnessed a pride of lions hunting in the middle of the day. It was my first time observing a hunt! I usually watched them eat their prey but had never been lucky enough to see them hunt. It was hard to watch, but it was an experience not to be missed. The hunt took quite a bit of time, and we needed to be extremely patient. The female lion went after a family of wildebeests, mostly attacking the baby. A few times, we could see the baby managing to run away and rejoining the family, only to get caught again by another lioness as we all watched, holding our breath, closing and opening our eyes in disbelief and horror. It was an awe-inspiring experience of watching life's most basic instinct: a true natural phenomenon.

Still high from the experience, we had a light picnic lunch where we sat around and asked the guide how often people got to see the migration. It was clear we were all worried, what if it didn't happen today or tomorrow while we were still in the park? Every year about a million wildebeest, half a million gazelles, and more than 200,000 zebra make the risky trek from Serengeti Park in Tanzania, to the Masai Mara Reserve

Abyssinian Nomad

in Kenya, in the search for water and food. It is one of nature's most spectacular sights and one that few people are lucky enough to witness firsthand.

Excited and anxious about our afternoon adventure in the park, we drove to the Mara River where the migration takes place. For many years, I had watched the migration on TV, but being there didn't seem real. As we approached the river, lo and behold, we saw the first brave wildebeests leaping into the river...

And then the magic happened. The stampede started, and the crocodiles' heads came out to snatch the unlucky ones. I couldn't look away as the ageless events unfolded before my eyes. Nothing in my life could compare with what I witnessed. I stood there, peering awestruck from the open-air roof of the game vehicle, with a sense of profound gratitude at being fortunate enough to witness this ancient African rite taking place before my very eyes. Though I might not know where I was going in life, I had come a long way.

Right next to us was a group of National Geographic reporters with large cameras who had been camping since the morning, waiting for the animals to cross. At least I now had an inkling of how long they had to wait, and I knew what it felt like to have watched the stampede live. With migration checked off, the hardest part of my travel was about to start.

One thing I love about couchsurfing is we never know what our experience will be when we meet or host or surfers. It's always a very unique and individual experience that makes my heart pump fast sometimes, just thinking about it. In this case, Kamau, my couchsurfing host in Nairobi, asked if I want to join him for lunch with his friends and their family to celebrate a young child's life that was taken away very early. I was touched by the story and agreed to join. The lunch was held at an upscale Nairobi restaurant's backyard filled with beautiful plants and flowers. There must have been about twenty-five to thirty affluent Kenyan family and friends, and I was not sure if there was anyone else there like me who crashed the party. Kamau kindly introduced me to his friends at the table we were sharing. To say the least, everyone was curious to know who I was. My host had recently moved back to Nairobi after over thirty years in the USA. We both explained about couchsurfing to his friends. While they didn't seem to understand it, they were very fascinated by my solo travel. While eating lunch and sharing stories, one of them, with great curiosity and bewilderment, turned to me and said, "So this thing works then?"

Me: "What thing?"

Him: "The internet thing?"

It was only then I understood, he was asking me if I'd met Kamau on a dating site and I was in Nairobi visiting him. We all laughed, once again trying to explain about couchsurfing.

At my request, Kamau also adopted for the next few days, my two travel partners until we could find a bus that would leave for Moyale on the Ethiopian border. The process of getting to Isiolo, the town where we could catch the horrifying bus that would take us on a bumpy and dusty road for over twelve hours, was as painful as the trip itself. No one knew when the bus was running—they said sometimes it was twice a week, sometimes three times, and sometimes not at all. Every day for almost for a week, we tried to buy tickets, but with no luck. Some people told us if we managed to go to Isiolo, we might be able to hitch a ride on a truck.

I had read different books, including guidebooks, that described that road trip as pure hell: dangerous roads, bandits, and the desert. To save my life, I wasn't going to brave hitchhiking on the back of a truck with cows, but my Japanese friends were ready to do it. With the help of a friend, we got a ride to Isiolo, where we crossed the equator. After taking pictures with the equator sign, there was nothing else to do.

We sat in a cafe, aimlessly waiting for a ride or the bus, anything that would get us to the border. It was difficult not to know when we would leave, but now and then we went out for a walk, where we were stormed by local kids and curious adults, mostly because of my Japanese friends.

We drank endless amounts of soft drinks and ate whatever we found. When it got dark, some trucks started to gather. Apparently, they came together to form a convoy, as the road was dangerous and they needed security to protect the goods or animals in the trucks. Some of the Somalis and Ethiopians we were hanging out with at the café, called people they knew and confirmed there would be a bus tonight. But all the trucks were leaving, and there was no sign of the bus. Though I had no idea where I would be spending the night, I was determined to wait. The bus finally showed up around midnight; it had broken down somewhere, and it had only a few passengers. I guess some people had already left using the trucks.

We said goodbye to the guys at the cafe, and boarded the bus. We took our backpacks on the bus with us, as some of the seats were empty, and we each took one row to stretch out and sleep. Sleep was difficult for me because of all the commotion about security and the talk of bandits shooting people on the buses. We were also told we would have armed men onboard throughout the bus ride; it sounded worse than what I'd read about.

Looking out the bus window, I would have to say the moon and stars shone more brightly than I had ever seen in my life. The sky looked magical as we drove into the darkness of the desert. The men armed with their AK47s stood inside the bus, looking out through the windows as if they could actually see anything and protect us from an attack. My friends were sleeping, but I was far from falling asleep. I sat there and witnessed the dawn breaking in the desert, while passing through a picturesque Turkana village.

Maskarm Haile

In the middle of nowhere, our bus broke down. It was already hot, and one tire had almost melted. There was no shade in sight and not much water to cool the engine either. The guys were hopeful that the bus would soon be fixed. Looking around, too hot to do anything, with nowhere to hide, I came face to face with my life. I had chosen to take that road trip knowing it would not be easy, but not realizing how difficult it would be. The fact I had come so far did not offer me any comfort; it was nerve-racking. We were stuck in the middle of nowhere. No one knew how long we would be there. We all had to depend on nature—there were no working phones and no villages to quickly run to. Everyone just sat or walked around, accepting what was. *Oh, traveling! The things you teach me.* Patience was never a virtue of mine, but in that situation, I definitely understood the value of it.

The bus broke down a few more times after that, and somehow, we arrived at a village where once again we had to pick up armed men. But that time one of them walked right to where I was sitting alone. My friends had decided to sleep, and there was a huge tire in the middle of the bus between us, so I couldn't quickly wake one of them. I saw that he was spaced out, his mouth filled with khat, and his lips looked like he was wearing green lipstick. In one hand was his gun and in the other a plastic bag filled with more khat. My heart sank.

I was sitting next to the window. Without even asking, the armed man sat in the middle seat next to me, casually acknowledging me, putting his AK47 between his legs and taking out more khat from his plastic bag. Knowing I was watching his every step, he offered me some, and I politely declined.

He was unmistakably Somalian, judging by his features, skin color, and the way he talked. My family and friends had pointed out lots of horrible scenarios when I started this journey, but none of them said I could be killed by an accidental gunshot on a bus. He was high, and I was not sure he knew what he was doing, or maybe he did. He tried to talk, but words failed him. I actually wanted him to speak to me so I could explain what I was doing and he would get to know me, and not try to kill me or do anything to me. But he couldn't talk! He suddenly put his hands on my thigh… I jumped.

It was pitch dark in the bus and outside, and most of the passengers were sleeping. My heart was beating so fast it felt like it had started its own orchestra. But he didn't react. I froze! I took his hands with both of mine and placed them on his lap, being as calm as I could and trying not to offend him. I was worried if he felt disrespected in any way, it wouldn't go too well. There was no way I wanted to hurt his ego—he was a man with AK47, and pretty high on khat in the middle of nowhere in Africa. Anything was possible.

I immediately started talking, asking if he was from Somalia and from which part. I told him how much I wanted to visit Somalia. On and on I went with no word from him. He just stared at me. I sensed he wasn't angry with me for moving his hand. When he finally tried to speak, he asked if he could share my water—I had my bottle beside me. I was willing to give him a bottle of Sprite I had that was warm, but wasn't opened. Something about that made him happy, I guess. He looked at me to say thank you and got up and left. I was shaken, and my mind couldn't stop replaying all the terrible things that could have happened. Once I realized the armed man was gone, my body started to shake, and my tears flowed involuntarily. That was a close call.

Chapter 22: The Spy with a Device

> *"The Danakil Depression in Ethiopia is home to the lowest point on Earth, Dallol, a lava lake that is 380 feet (116 m) below sea level. It is also one of the only lava lakes in the world, and it is the hottest place on the planet."*
> *~ 67 interesting facts about Ethiopia*

DON'T GO TO ETHIOPIA IF you are a solo woman traveler. That was the message on the travel blogs I read. Even a couple of couchsurfers who didn't know I was Ethiopian had warned me, saying Ethiopia is not suitable for women travelers. I politely replied to the emails saying thank you for the tips and information, but I was determined to find out for myself. And I would always add: "And PS, I am Ethiopian."

I was exhausted and worn out when I crossed the border into Ethiopia. I wanted some information from locals. At that point, I was very disappointed and frustrated with my guidebook. The big Lonely Planet guidebook I had been carrying around was of no use when it came to small towns. The places mentioned in the guide were often closed, or the Lonely Planet printed outdated information every year. Many times, I wanted to scream and send the editors of the Lonely Planet emails, complaining about the inaccuracies.

At the border, I met a couple of young men who were waiting for tourists, hoping to act as tour guides to earn quick money. One of them in particular was very happy to find out I was Ethiopian, doing what he thought only white people did. I was very conscious talking to him and his friends at the beginning when they surrounded us. Naturally, their target was my Japanese friends. They wanted to sell them local currency, accommodation, tours—anything. Unfortunately for him, my friends were budget travelers. However, he insisted, saying all he wanted to do was help me. Indeed, he was my angel: he explained the best way to catch the bus to Yabelo, which was complicated by the sporadic bus schedule.

Dreading another five-hour bus ride on a "chicken bus" (a crowded bus with people, goods, and animals) without having had a shower, I reluctantly agreed to the idea. It was one of the best decisions I made on my trip. The young man made sure I got a seat on the bus, ran to the store and got me water, and introduced me to the driver, his assistant, and a young man who was also on the bus. They were all super-friendly, and I felt welcomed already. The bus didn't leave immediately, but the assistant gave up his front seat for me and my backpack. My Japanese friends couldn't make up their minds if they were going to go to Boerne (where the market was the next day) or Yabelo. They were also hoping to be hosted by locals in the village.

I wanted a shower and a clean bed, and I saw there was one hotel in Yabelo, a little upscale, about US $20-30 a night, but I didn't mind paying a little extra for one night. I explained to the driver and his assistant that I needed to be dropped off at the hotel in town. They knew the place and offered me a ride to the market in Borena the next day. It all sounded great. My friends met a family on the bus and decided to get off in Borena. I knew we would keep bumping into each other for the next few days because we were there to do the same thing: go see the market and explore the southern tribes.

When we finally reached the one-and-only Yabelo hotel, I found out the UN was organizing a big peace meeting with the nearby tribal leaders, because apparently, there was some tension in the area. Every room was taken! I didn't know what to do. The driver and his assistant didn't know what to do with me, either. They obviously didn't want to leave me and go away. It was almost dark, and the young man, the tour guide, who turned out to be the owner of the bus, suggested I come with them and he would find me a safe place for the night. They might even be able to get me a bucket of water to wash.

He was sure it would be better than where they were staying, so I agreed and followed the three men. The place was a small shack, at the back of a bar or a restaurant. I had no idea which was worse—the night bus in the middle of a desert, or a night in a shack in a middle of nowhere. But, I was grateful to those men; they had taken it upon themselves to make sure I was safe. The young man brought the owner outside to introduce me, and I was taken to the back door to the room. For some reason, they didn't want people to see me enter. It was probably the shadiest and most nerve-racking place I had stayed so far.

The door barely seemed to lock, but seeing the owner and the guys all confident, I thought it should be okay. After all, I didn't have any other choice. I was asked to pay 20 Birr, about US $1. They quickly explained it was a little more because I asked for water. One of the employees brought a small bucket of water. It was cold, but I was just so grateful to have water that would wash away the dust. I was even more grateful for my sleeping bag. I slept like a baby.

Abyssinian Nomad

When the guys came in the morning to pick me up, I was in a good mood. They were like my chaperones: I would be going around with them as they picked up passengers to take to the market. But before that, we went for breakfast, which was fresh meat (siga tibs). There was nothing else in town. So, I ate with them, knowing it would probably be the only fresh food I would find the whole day.

When we arrived in Borana, the first thing I wanted to do was see "The Singing Well." The well describes the life of the Borana people, a semi-nomadic shepherds' tribe. The ancient hand-excavated wells are managed by the shepherds, and every day the young shepherds form human chains to reach the depths of the well and collect water while chanting.

Amman, the young owner of the bus, was fascinated by my traveling and determination to see the places, so he decided to come along. "The Singing Well" was one of the favorite tourist activities, and easy to find. But the locals found it funny that we were going to see the well because we were Ethiopians. Amman had been working in that area for years, but he had never gone to see it. When we got there, there were guys making a line by standing one above the other on the stairs, and tossing up the water in the buckets from person to person while singing a song to honor their cattle.

The Borana market was open and vibrant, and as I'd expected, I ran into Satomi and Akio in the market. It was a happy and hug-filled moment when we saw each other. I told them where I ended up staying. They were satisfied with their stay with the family and loved the little kids in the house.

While on the way back to Yabelo, Amman told me he had rented his bus to transport some of the UN and tribal leaders to a different meeting place the next day, and he would ask the manager if I could go with them. If it worked out, not only would I get a ride to Jinka, but I could meet lots of locals from different tribes and also visit some amazing places with them.

Maskarm Haile

The people were so kind and happy to have me around. It was touching to see how they reacted to my presence. Most invited me to their village, to visit their family, and to stay with them for as long as I liked. So, over the next few days, we visited more markets, the famous Omo River, and the Karo and Hummer tribes.

When we got to the Hummer village, Amman and I met a very enthusiastic child who spoke a little Amharic in the village. We walked around the village, visiting the homes and families of locals we'd met in the market. Drinking coffee, the children combed my hair and wondered why I looked so different from them. The women laughed when I told them I didn't have kids. It was indeed an amazing experience being with them.

Word had gone around about an Ethiopian tourist (me), and the tour guides were curious about me. I was also looking for a ride to visit the Mursi village and to possibly go to Addis in the next few days.

One of the NGO managers who had rented Amman's bus had brought his two kids. I had been talking to them when we were in the market, and they had told their father they wanted to go with me to the Mursi village. They had a 4X4 with a driver, and the family confirmed they wanted to tour the Mago National Park. I agreed to pay my share of the gas. We got caught in heavy rain which lasted the entire night and the following day. The driver was concerned, saying he had heard the road was dangerous. It was only the kids and me who wanted to go no matter what. As usual, the bureaucracy was endless. We needed to get a pass to go into the park. It was not the standard park fee, but we needed some kind of permit from the region first, and when we asked where the park management office was to pay the fee, they said we needed to go make a 25km off-road detour from where we were going.

Abyssinian Nomad

The rain was getting stronger, and driving was becoming impossible. The driver was unhappy, as we had taken the off-road turn to pay the park fees. I was annoyed because of the lack of information, and that the park management made it hard for the tourists and the tour companies to pay the fee.

Suddenly the car spun and got stuck in the mud. The driver's worst fears had been confirmed; we were stuck and could be there for days on end. The truth was, yes, we were off-road, and we had heard that some of the tour guides got their permits in advance, as it took so much out of their day. So, unless there were people like us on a private tour, no one was going to come our way.

I suggested we walk to the main road and get help. The family had come to the park because of me, and now it was clear they were starting to regret it. I jumped out of the car and walked to the main road. When I got to the main road, there weren't any passing cars, but I saw two men as drenched as I was walking toward me in the rain. The looks on their faces were priceless, checking me out from head to foot, with my light rain jacket and bare feet standing by the side of the street.

I said, "Hello." And then I started telling them how our car was stuck a few meters away from where I was standing and asked if they could help us pull it out. No answer… When they finally decided to talk to me, of course, we didn't speak the same language. It reminded me of one of the emails I had received at the beginning of my travels. I had been asking other travelers about tips and information, and someone had sent me a long email with all the useful advice and suggestions, but had signed off saying I had nothing to worry about since I speak African.

African?

There I was in the country of my birth, and I wasn't even able to communicate with a fellow Ethiopian to save my life.

Maskarm Haile

The men were kind and followed me to the car and helped us get the vehicle out of the mud. At this point, there was no reason to be upset about what had happened. We were all cold, wet, and entirely covered in mud. I was just happy that we were on our way. When we got to the entrance to the park, there was confusion and a lengthy discussion of how much the park officials should charge me. Should they give me the Ethiopian rate or the foreigner (Ferengi) price?

By the time we got to the park, other cars had already started to arrive. We were a bunch of people who had traveled from far and wide to see the Mursi tribe, mostly known as the "lip plate tribe" due to their large, clay lip plates in their faces. They live a simple life; it's only in recent years they have been visited by tourists.

For years it had been one of my dreams to visit the Omo valley region, mostly because of the photos we saw in school that showed the diverse tribes around Ethiopia. Most of the tribes in that region are considered Africa's last tribes, and it was a huge privilege and incredible feeling to stand in the national park among the Mursi.

For the women, the process of wearing those large plates starts at the age of fifteen, where their bottom lips are sliced and small plates are placed to grow the piercing over the years. Same with their ear piercing. To them, it is a sign of beauty, and it brings a great reward when they marry by bringing more cattle as dowry. Not only that, but the Mursi women decorate their bodies by using the needles of the acacia tree to make designs and letting the wounds heal as raised scars.

The men, on the other hand, usually get scars for the enemies they kill, showing them off openly as medals.

Sadly, because of tourism, the tribes are relying on the money they get for pictures from tourists, which is causing them to be labeled as aggressive. Though the experience was priceless, it was also hard for me to witness a kind of human safari. There was no time for them to see us as anything other than a money-making machine—and for us to see them as a trophy to take a photo of.

There were tourists from every part of the world. As much as I had wanted this trip for so long and I was happy to be there, I quickly lost the excitement of this particular experience. For me, traveling was all about connecting with people. Here at the Mursi village, I felt like an uninvited guest.

Once again, in the middle of the Mursi village, I ran into my Japanese friends. They had hitched a ride with two British guys, Kasper and Chris, who had been traveling in Ethiopia for three weeks. I briefly talked to them, and we decided to have drinks that evening when we got back to Jinka, where we would all be spending the night.

That time I was staying in a relatively good place, so I could at least look forward to a shower. The man who gave me a lift to the park and his children were super-happy that they had decided to come with me. The kids thanked me, and their father was also glad to see the tribe. I didn't want to spoil the fun by sharing what I felt. I just went along with their happiness.

Back in the hotel in Jinka, it was time to find another ride to Addis. On the main market day, I met lots of tour guides, some of whom were very kind and understanding. Kasper and Alex, who had given a lift to my Japanese friends, told me at dinner that they needed to head back to Addis soon because they were flying out. So we agreed to meet up in the town of Arba Minch in two days.

When we were discussing the plans, the driver or tour guide wasn't with them, but I assumed it would be fine since they were paying for the car. They had rented the car for three weeks, and they could give a ride to anyone they wanted. But there was a huge problem I didn't know about. The tour company they'd hired online for three weeks and paid in advance, now had them pay more money, saying the price of fuel had increased. The driver was also making them pay extra for his food and accommodation, claiming they were responsible for him once they were on the road.

The next day I took a bus to Arba Minch to spend some time at the lake, as I was craving some quiet time on my own before going back to Addis. Things had been happening so quickly since I'd crossed into Ethiopia. I wanted to reflect on my decisions. Though I had no idea where my life was going, I was happy to start feeling alive and connected again. I found a nice clean place in Arba Minch where the family was kind and thoughtful. They held a coffee ceremony, inviting me to their house even though they didn't understand what a woman like me was doing on the road on her own.

Over coffee and popcorn, the ladies interrogated me, laughing at times, and also were very concerned about me. They were fascinated when I told them my boyfriend Jules was Canadian. They nodded their heads as if they had found the clue and said it was no wonder I was free to travel the way I was. They laughed about the men they knew; one of them even told me she couldn't even say hello to another man without her husband getting jealous. Another confirmed that she too didn't like it when her husband talked to other women. It was all "girly" and light; I really enjoyed my afternoon with the ladies. That evening I walked around the town and wrote in my journal. It was a freezing night, but I managed to sleep well.

The next day after breakfast, Kasper and Alex called to let me know they were in town. I explained where I was staying to the driver and they came and picked me up. Once I was in the car, barely finishing my greetings, I saw the driver looking at me. He said to me in Amharic that I needed to pay him extra. Not understanding what was going on, I asked whether I was paying or sharing costs. If so, I would pay Kasper and Alex and not him. Our conversation alarmed them. Alex was in the front seat, looking very unhappy, and Kasper was talking most of the time. He explained that Alex was exhausted and pissed off and he didn't want to lose his temper. Three weeks of dealing with the driver and the tour company had left them feeling exploited. And if that weren't bad enough, the driver wanted more money from me. I realized that it was going to be a long drive.

The driver was upset with me for telling them he wanted money. He started talking to me in Amharic. Those fantastic men, Amman, his driver and assistant, had driven me around for the last two weeks but never took a cent from me, and I had experienced the utmost kindness from them. I knew this driver was being a greedy jerk. I was in the middle of nowhere and couldn't get out of the car. So, I agreed to pay the 500 Birr he wanted, and I told the guys not to worry about it. We all knew that it was wrong, but I didn't want to fight over it.

The driver was also angry that my Japanese friends hadn't paid him, and he wanted me to pay for them too. I tried to explain there were lots of people traveling like us, hitchhiking and staying with locals, and we didn't have a lot of money. We were budget travelers. He wanted to know why we came to visit if we didn't have the money to rent our own guides. But he didn't stop there—he felt the need to give me advice and said that as a woman I should just stay at home and watch National Geographic, and that I shouldn't be wandering around. All of it was said in Amharic.

I was furious! No words could describe what I felt at that moment. I almost yelled at him and explained to Kasper and Alex what he had just said to me. He was a tour guide, making a living out of tourists, and yet he was telling me to watch National Geographic... He was not only greedy but also heartless and apparently unable to see the fallacy of his argument and how that would impact his livelihood. Luckily, I had experienced enough generosity in Ethiopia from total strangers to know he was just a bad apple.

After a quick visit to the crocodile farm, we hit the road. Now and then we told the guide to drive slowly, but he didn't listen. It was as if he had hired us all to work for him, rather than him driving the car for us. As he was also making plans with his friend for khat when he got to Addis, he was in a hurry to get back. When we stopped for lunch, we told him again to slow down—we had seen all kinds of overturned vehicles by the side of the roads.

When we said we wanted to stop to see the places along the way, he freaked out. It was also clear we wouldn't be making it to Addis unless we drove through the night, and we didn't want to do that. Driving with the guide during the day was traumatic enough. When we reached the Konso region, it was getting late, so we again asked him again to find a decent place for us. Completely ignoring us, he continued driving.

Finally, after it got dark and we were in the middle of nowhere, he started to look for accommodation. We had passed all the places that looked like towns. He stopped at a building that was still under construction, jumped out of the car and went inside, and came out with another person to offload our backpacks, announcing that was where we would be staying for the night.

The man said we were to pay 30 Birr or US $1.50 for the night. He said there was water and a toilet. We went inside only to find that the place wasn't even finished: it was pure cement, freezing cold, with no running water and only a few beds in some unfinished rooms. The guys were given one room, and I had my own.

I was both outraged and sad that he was treating us like that, and I didn't understand why he decided to be so exploitative toward me. It wasn't fair treating people who had spent so much of their money to come and visit his beautiful country the way he did. It felt like we were hostages for some crime we didn't know about. They wanted us to pay the money and treated us as if we were going to run away with it. We paid; I seem to recall that we also had to pay for him. We went to our cold rooms and spent a sleepless night.

When we got up in the morning still traumatized, the guide came to me and said that I should please tell my friends there was a misunderstanding last night about the price of the room. It was US $30 and not 30 Birr. So far, I had tried not to take sides and had stopped myself from saying anything to him or to them, but as we had our backpacks and were coming out of that unfinished place, I lost it.

I said, "No. No, I am not going to translate for you. And no. We are not paying one extra penny for you or anyone else." Seeing me furious, Kasper walked to me and asked what was going on. So I told him what the guide had said, and I said it was up to him what he decided, but it was insane to ask for so much money. By then we were surrounded by people, and the guide was telling me if we didn't pay he would have to pay from his pocket, and his family wouldn't have food to eat. We put our backpacks on and got in the car. Kasper and Alex refused to pay, too.

The guide got in the car cursing and yelling, mostly at me. As if I was supposed to understand and take pity on him. He argued that it was because of me that he lost US $60. I didn't care. My 20 Birr room in Yabelo was a lot better value for the money than that place. Thanking Kasper and Alex and wishing them a great flight, I got out of the car in Addis Ababa. It had been a hellish drive. Everything could have been avoided, the guide could have been fantastic, and gotten tips from all of us and maybe even recommendations.

Being back in Addis Ababa for the first time without my mother was very hard. Every time I crossed a border I had to fight the urge to call her. Now that I was more than halfway through my journey and was in my home country, it was even harder for me to bear my loss. My mother used to listen to my stories even if she never understood what I was talking about or I sounded crazy. She tried to be interested. My father and the rest of the family only knew when I was back or when I had gone again. Nevertheless, they were happy to see me. Some of my friends were still around and made sure they hung out with me when I was visiting, even going to the extent of attending the couchsurfing meetups I organized while in town. Later, they would tell me how crazy I was, or how much they hated it. Though it was sometimes offensive, I understood that I was the one forcing the idea of connecting people. Most were happy (at least they seemed happy) living life the way they believed was right for them.

Jules was thrilled when I finally saw him. I felt remorse as I didn't feel the same anymore, and had got over the idea of pleasing my dead mother. But I tried to see the relationship beyond my mom's wish for me to be married by asking myself if it was what I really and truly wanted to do.

Jules and I hung out for a few weeks and talked for hours. Jules was a regular at my dad's house, but he had rented a house, and he wanted me to be there with him all the time. I wanted to spend time with my father, and also meet up with my friends before I set off again, but it became an impossible mission without making Jules feel abandoned.

My Japanese friends came to visit as I had promised to host them at my father's house. I had already told him that my friends were coming for few days. When they arrived, my father seemed happy; I guess he was just happy having me around. My parents were used to me bringing or sending people to their house way before couchsurfing, so nothing surprised them—except when my Japanese friends arrived at our house and told me they had a few more friends from Japan arriving on a flight the next day. Already Satomi and

Abyssinian Nomad

Akio were sleeping on the floor in the living room downstairs, and my father felt sorry that they were sleeping on a mattress. Little did he know where and how we had slept before. I agreed to host the rest of the Japanese crew--we had extra mattresses and couches, and it would be okay. At least it was clean and safe, and there was water (but that really depended on the day). I forgot to tell my father three more Japanese guests were coming, and he woke up to find five people sleeping on the floor in the living room. I guess that day my dad gave up the idea that things about me would change.

In an attempt to cheer up Jules and make him warm to the idea of couchsurfing, my Japanese friends decided to make Japanese food with all the fresh ingredients the newcomers had brought from Japan. Jules offered them his place to cook and stay the night. It was one of the most delightful evenings we had had, drinking matcha tea, eating Japanese snacks and food. My obsession with Japanese food and drink needs a book of its own—I was in heaven.

Akio and Satomi and their friends from Japan were supposed to travel through Ethiopia while I sorted out my life in Addis and my next destination. We planned to meet again to head to the north to Sudan.

In the meantime, I had also tried to make a quick trip to Afar to see the active volcano and the lowest place on Earth, Dallol. I had heard how hard it was to get there, but I was willing to try. So, I called a tour company recommended by an online forum.

When a man answered, I introduced myself and politely enquired about their Afar tour. He was kind enough to explain the packages they had, and then he asked how many Ferengis there were. I suddenly realized he had assumed I was calling on behalf of some tourists. I said it was for me and I was interested in joining a group if they already had one. There was a long pause, and I could hear his breathing from the other end. I explained how much I wanted to do the tour, but it was time sensitive. When he finally spoke, I could hear his disappointment. He said he would call me back and let me know, but I never heard from him.

The weeks flew by fast, and I was afraid to tell my father I was going to Somalia and Somaliland. Somehow, I gathered my courage to tell Jules the relationship wasn't working for me. I said I was sorry and acknowledged how wrong I was to start a relationship when I knew the journey I was on was very important to me. I was the girl from Ethiopia who had a dream, and my dream to travel the world came true not because I had money, but because of the people I met around the world who opened their houses and hearts. I would be forever indebted to the hundreds of people who talked to me, smiled at me, took me to their homes, gave me rides, fed me and washed my laundry. So, I was not going to impose that on someone else who felt so distant and was happy just doing his bit in the world. I wasn't happy breaking up. But I knew it would save us a lot of heartache in the future.

I also found the courage to tell my father I was planning to go to Somalia and Somaliland. He was quiet, numb; I'm sure he was worried about the situation there. He had not said much since my mother's death. I felt his pain, and the last thing I wanted to do was inflict more suffering on him, but as I was there, I felt he deserved to know. Usually, my siblings and I told our mother everything, and she was the one who broke it to him. He hardly talked to us on the phone. My father and my conversations never went past the stage of, "How are you? Is everything okay? Do you need anything? Okay, talk to your mother!"

My father would now have to have a conversation with me. Neither of us had a choice but to try to communicate the best way we could. My policy was to tell him the truth, but he didn't respond well. He said "Okay," but I didn't understand what that okay meant, whether it was sincere, or if he was unhappy with my decision. I always knew where I stood with my mother. With my father, it would be a process where we would need to learn to communicate. He didn't have my mother anymore to hand over the phone to.

When I went to the Somali Embassy, I was told I would need private security the whole time I would be in Mogadishu. One of the people at the consulate in Addis was so impressed that I wanted to visit that he was willing to organize the security himself for me. I knew I was crazy, but it didn't feel right going into Mogadishu, Somalia. I thought of how my father would be affected if anything happened to me in Somalia. I also wondered why I was doing what I was doing. My dream wasn't about touching the land for the sake of counting countries. My desire to travel was way more than just being in a new country; it was about experiencing life with locals. I didn't think the locals would have the time or the desire to explore a life and traveling when bombs were being thrown at them.

I was still sitting at the consulate having tea with the employees when the secretary walked in and asked for my photos. I had left them at home while I was changing my bag. I remembered telling myself that I needed them, but then left them on the side table. Feeling a little relieved, I walked out of the embassy, and later called the man who'd promised to organize security for me and tell him that I changed my mind about going to Somalia.

The next day, I went to get my Somaliland visa and booked my flight to Jijiga, a small town close to the border, to save time. I had wasted lots of time and was afraid to tell my father again that I was going. I was also scared to mention the breakup with Jules. As I wanted to meet up with my Japanese friends heading north, flying was the only option. Plus, I had visited the eastern part of Ethiopia with my mother when I was young, and it would be a painful memory. I was consciously doing everything I could to avoid pain.

I did everything the Lonely Planet Guide told me to do when I got to Jijiga. Though Somaliland was considered safer than Somalia, it was still a no-go territory for travelers. There was still war in the area near Al Shabaab, and Somaliland was not yet recognized as a country by the UN. The Lonely Planet admirably said it was okay to go out, but I had to make sure to stay in the one-and-only big, expensive hotel for security. I thought I could do that; I had lots of fantastic Somalian friends over the years and had come to love their sense of community, openness, kindness, and fearlessness about life. I was also drawn to their nomadic lifestyle. One day they would be here, and the next they would be miles away, and that was normal for them. I had friends who never moved apartments in the same city, while my Somalian friends changed countries or even continents. I wished I had Somalian blood in my family so my lifestyle could be justified, and my family and their friends would feel at peace with my lifestyle.

I took the bus to the border. It was excruciatingly hot and dry, and the vegetation was very dry. I was once again feeling happy and free in my soul to be back on the road. However, my body was tired, maybe from a combination of things. I felt like I was coming down with some kind of cold or flu and had a slight fever and cough. I told myself it was not a good time to be sick, not then and not anytime soon, as I still had a few more countries left to visit to make my dream come true.

But my body didn't listen, and no amount of Tylenol was going to get rid of my fever. Still, I took the bus and headed for the border, but by the time we got there, I had a full-blown cold, chills in my body, and was feeling very weak.

The Ethiopian customs checkpoint was a few kilometers before the Somaliland border. We all had to get off the bus as instructed with our belongings. One man approached me asking me for my identity card, so I took out my passport and gave it to him. He went through it, page by page. Wondering what he was looking for, I explained I had my Ethiopian multiple visa entry and tried to show the stamps from Moyale. Little did I know that by mentioning Moyale, I'd make them suspect me as a spy.

The immigration officer called his friends over and told them I must be a Canadian or American spy, trying to fool them. Politely I told them I speak Amharic and understood what they were saying. I said I wasn't a spy. Feeling both offended and proud for catching me, one of the guys ordered a complete search of my backpack. By then the search for the rest of the passengers on the bus was almost over, and the people started circling us. He called the woman officer to go through my stuff. She began to throw my things onto the ground. But then she saw my passport bag in my hand—she thought I was going to hide it from her. She snatched it out of my hand and started opening it. I had about US $200, Canadian$20, €20, and some other currencies that I had been collecting as souvenirs. She called her colleagues to confirm that I was a spy because of the foreign currency I was carrying.

I tried to reason with her. Luckily, I had a receipt from the ATM in Addis that showed I had made a cash withdrawal in Ethiopian Birr and I wasn't selling or buying on the black market. And also, as I was traveling, I needed to keep some cash with me, but it was the money I brought into the country. There was a big commotion, and the bus driver came to tell me that if I wasn't back in five minutes he would leave without me. The officers were quick to comment and said I wasn't going anywhere. Looking at him, wordlessly I begged the driver. No one was getting on the bus; they were all giving their opinion. All I heard was, "Ay, America!"

While the men were arguing over whether to give me my money back, the woman opened my toilet bag and grabbed a bunch of tampons and screamed loudly to the officers, saying that she had found the device! And she handed them each a few. She had her evidence that I was a spy.

There was more commotion. One of the officers told the people to get back on the bus, and I stood there trying to figure out what just happened. She had handed my tampons to the men, and I knew that when they realized what they were, they were going to be even more offended. She wouldn't listen to me, so I grabbed her hand as if hoping that by shaking her, I would snap her out of her fantasy about catching an American/Canadian spy at the Ethiopian border. I said to her that she had given the men my tampons. But looking at her face, I saw she didn't understand what I said; she kept on talking about "the device" (the only English words she used). I shook her again and explained what a tampon is used for.

Time stood still for a second, and then she screamed out, "*Beshmaa ab weld*" and made the sign of the cross on her face. She was disgusted by what I had said. She didn't want to touch any of my things anymore and told me to get out of her sight. With half of my belongings hanging out of my backpack, I ran to the bus just as the driver was starting to drive away. I frantically checked and made sure I had my passport with me. It was the only thing I was worried about. I knew when the male officers found out what they were holding in their hands, they would be angry with me. Later, when I flew out, I was worried the security would not let me through. Fortunately, I found out they weren't Immigration officers. It was just a checkpoint to make sure people didn't smuggle goods out of Ethiopia.

Chapter 23: Saved by the Brother

*"Somaliland, officially the Republic of Somaliland,
is a self-declared state, internationally recognized as an
autonomous region of Somalia."*
~ Wikipedia

ONCE I CLEARED THE BORDER, I took a taxi and paid for both myself and my backpack to sit in the front seat. Yes, if you want to take your bags with you, you need to pay extra in some parts of Africa.

I was sick. The taxi ride to Hargeisa felt very long, and I could hardly wait to get to the hotel to sleep. As soon as we got into town, the taxi driver said we had reached the drop-off. I asked if he could take me the hotel mentioned in the guidebook, but he said that he had something else to do. I love how Somalians can be so unapologetic, but at the time it was a huge inconvenience.

I saw a small cafe at the side of the street. I walked in and sat down in the small garden and ordered tea and some Miranda (a soft drink). I needed a miracle to get me to the hotel. At that point, I didn't even know how far away it was, and I didn't see any people or transport nearby. I was coughing quite hard and felt as if I would fall asleep where I was sitting, but I took out my guidebook in the hope that maybe when I got some energy, I would ask the man at the cafe where to find a taxi or to even call one for me. Kids started to gather around me, dancing around my backpack and chair.

I noticed a man with a hat, sitting and quietly reading a newspaper. Some of the children realized I was Ethiopian and tried to talk to me, but I didn't understand what they were saying. I finally asked the kids if they knew where the taxi stop was. I thought the word "taxi" would be readily understood, and they would be able to tell me. Then I saw the man with the hat look up and face me. In perfect English, he asked if I was waiting for someone at the taxi stop. Perhaps some family or friends who would come to pick me up, because lots of Ethiopians went there to welcome their family or friends who were looking for work in the new country.

I was feeling very sick at that point, but knowing the man spoke English made me think I would be just fine. I was sure he would know the hotel and where to get a taxi at least. I said the name of the hotel and asked him if he could help me get there.

He walked to my table and asked why I wanted to go there—it was far and expensive. I explained the Lonely Planet Guidebook mentioned that for women solo travelers, it was their best bet to stay safe in the country. He smiled and said not to worry. He would walk me to a nice hotel in the town and would make sure I'd be okay.

I summoned up all my energy and got out of my chair, putting my backpack on my back. When my new friend saw what I was wearing, he said that first I needed a dress, then medicine and then a SIM card for my phone. In that order. Women were not permitted to walk around in Somaliland in trousers. As we started walking, with me giving thanks and counting my blessings, I found out that my new friend, Mohamed, was from Toronto and he had moved back after the formation of Somaliland. He was a brother, I thought, almost wanting to jump up and down. That perfect stranger was my brother, bonded by a faraway land we both call home. We both beamed as if we had known each other for ages.

I wore a scarf that covered my hair, but people started to stare at me because I was wearing trousers. He said I should not worry about them because I was with him for today. We stopped at the hotel first. It was right on the market and the owner came out to greet us.

Apparently, the owner had moved back from the US. He had a few Ethiopians working in his hotel, and he said I would feel right at home. He also called one of the women to go with us to help me buy a long dress. But I said it was okay, I wasn't planning on spending a lot of time shopping. All I wanted was just to get a long dress—I wouldn't be able to rest if I didn't buy one. As we reached the market, the man in the hat went to greet a female tailor and asked her if she had anything ready-made. Unfortunately, she didn't, but she said she could make a dress in half an hour and send it to my hotel. I quickly gave her my room number.

On my way back to my hotel, we stopped at the local pharmacy and got some cold and cough medication and a SIM card just in case I needed to call anyone later if I didn't feel better.

Once I had everything I needed, Mohamed walked me back to my hotel and left, saying he would be back the next day with his wife to check on me.

I bought a couple of bottles of water and some Miranda and went up to my room, where I took the vitamin C, cold and flu medicine, and cough syrup and put on every item of clothing I had. Thinking it would be hot, I hadn't really brought much with me. Then I passed out.

Maskarm Haile

I woke up in the middle of the night feeling disoriented. I had no idea where I was. I looked at my pillows and bed cover as if they could tell me something. But for the life of me, I couldn't remember where I was. In a panic, I sat up on my bed. There wasn't much light in the room, but the light from the main road shone a little, and I tried to figure out where I was and in whose house, which hotel and which country. I told myself to stay calm and tried to track my day from what I remembered. Oh. I was in a taxi, plane, bus, taxi, and I remember being sick, the checkpoint in Ethiopia, the man I met at the cafe…

Phew, that was scary. It was still daylight when I went to bed, so I hadn't oriented myself with the light switches, and I also hadn't taken out my flashlight from my bag. But the good news was I didn't have a high fever and I wasn't feeling congested anymore. I crawled to my backpack and found my flashlight; I was curious what my room looked like.

When I woke up in the morning, I was feeling much better and excited to be there. When I called the reception, I found my dress was waiting for me. But I had no idea what I was going to do or where I was going—nothing! I just wanted to be there. I had been inspired by the Somalians' sense of freedom; I wanted to see them, and how they lived in their own country. Mohamed was a testament to that. I really hoped he would come around so I could hear his story. What brought him back to Somalia? Wasn't life in Toronto much better than the dusty Hargeisa?

While having breakfast at the hotel, my phone rang. It was Mohamed. Yay! He asked how I was and what I planned to do. I had no plans. Zero! But how could I tell him that when I said I was a tourist, and all I wanted to do was walk around, drink tea and chat with locals? I knew that where there was khat, there was also tea. But something else came out of my mouth: I said I wanted to see the market. Mohamed answered that his wife and her sister were coming to my hotel to take me shopping. He obviously didn't want to get involved with shopping, and I guess he understood I wanted to shop.

The two ladies looked amazing in their headscarves and long dresses. Oh, the colors! There was something different about Somalians; the women were tall with beautiful skin color. But that wasn't the only thing that made me fall in love with them—Somalian women were fearless, they walked with their heads held high wherever they went. They knew how to get things done. Their voices might be quiet, but they could also be loud. They could make the ground shake if they wanted. I was happy to hang out with those ladies.

Just outside the hotel in the open market, the first thing I noticed was vendors exchanging stacks of money on the street as if they were selling fresh produce. There were piles and piles of money in wheelbarrows and just simply on the ground. There weren't any security guards or guns. People were walking around doing their thing, and the men were counting. The bank was open for business. Seeing me staring and watching in disbelief, the ladies thought I wanted to exchange my hard currency, but I had already done that at the hotel earlier in the morning. I had never been anywhere where money was traded on the black market in barrels, and on the floor like that, not in Africa nor anywhere else in the world. I thought they must have felt quite safe. I had been worried to tell people I was going to Somaliland because it was dangerous, but people were exchanging money on the street.

The gold souks were busy, and people bought gold like they bought their groceries. When I asked why they did that, I was told that women love gold. I hardly saw any men with jewelry. I was busy looking at the women in colorful clothes and head covers. The traditional attire of the Somalian women is very diverse, influenced by religion, age, region, and the occasion. The women also told me something I would have never known: Somalian women were as obsessed with curtains and carpets as they were with beautiful garments and gold.

It was wonderful hanging out with those lovely ladies, but I didn't buy anything as the little fancy shops weren't for me. I wanted to trade the air-conditioning for the bustling, hot, and chaotic open markets. I appeared to be walking with a purpose, as if I knew what I was doing, but truly I was spaced out. Deep inside me, I was ecstatic. I was home! Not home in a conventional way, but I liked it there and I wanted to stay. I felt the heartbeat of the place; people screamed in a language I didn't speak; the music blared out of old speakers, and the sun beat down on my head. My soul felt free, and once again, I felt at one with everything, including the dust I was chewing at that point.

When I got back to my hotel feeling dizzy from my excitement, Mohamed and his friends were waiting for me. They seemed to be happy and proud of me. He had told them about me, and I guess they wanted to come and see for themselves. They were all from the USA, Canada, and the UK, but they had chosen to come back and live in Somaliland. I admired their courage but could never do it myself. They were quick to admit that it wasn't easy for women to live there, especially women who came back from the West. We then went to eat some delicious local food.

Over the meal, I told my friends how I used to go to the Somalian restaurant on Bloor Street in Toronto years back. He said he also used to hang out there with his friends as a young man. We both laughed. It was incredible how small things can become bonding instruments, bringing pure joy.

When I mentioned I wanted to see the Berbera Port, they said I needed not only a car but also an armed guard. My mind flashed back to the bus in Kenya, and I instantly felt sick—a man with an AK47 in a bus. But I had heard so much about it when I was growing up that I wanted to see it. The guys promised to find me someone they knew and trusted to accompany me. Though I didn't like the idea of having someone with a gun in the car with me, it was a law in the country: all tourist leaving the city of Hargassa must always be accompanied by armed security. I sat at the back of the car while the driver and the security guard who never spoke a word of English chatted all the way to Barbara. I didn't mind at all. I was just happy staring outside the window, finally get to see the place I heard so much about.

I had come a long way in creating a Somalian family in Somaliland! My gratitude was immense.

Chapter 24: Undercover Police

"Sudan used to be the largest country in Africa and the Middle East (area wise), before the country split in two in July 2011 (Sudan and South Sudan)."
~ Interesting facts about Sudan

GETTING A SUDANESE VISA IS not one of the easiest things to do in Addis. But once you do get it, it's like walking around with a time bomb in your hand. I had to leave Addis right away because the validity of the visa started from the day it was issued. If you were flying and had your ticket ready, it would work. But if you are taking a bus and want to stop in every village, it won't be so easy. Sudan is a big country, and the visa I got was only for two weeks. To be specific, it was a two weeks' transit visa.

Leaving Addis Ababa that time was very emotional, after having been in Africa for almost two years, going to Addis as often as I did, and staying even longer when my mom passed. Not only did it bring back lots of emotions, but it also posed some serious questions. As a little girl, I had two big dreams. Nothing complicated: I wanted to travel the world, and I wanted to make a difference in people's lives. These goals had been my driving force for everything I had done in my life. As much as I was traveling, I was also trying different ways make a difference in people's lives, volunteering in shelters, hospitals, and schools. I even went to Cotonou, Benin, in West Africa to volunteer for six months.

But knowing and understanding what fulfillment feels like, I knew some aspects of my life still needed a little more soul-searching. And even though I had made one of my dreams come true, I was feeling even more guilty—there was so much more I could share and do with the world.

I wasn't sure if I wanted to go back to Ethiopia or anywhere else in Africa for a while. With my mother gone, I thought Africa and I could use a little break from each other. So not knowing when I would see my family and friends again, my goodbyes were bittersweet.

On my last day, after saying goodbye to everyone, I went to stay with a local couchsurfer, Mika. We had met a few times already, and I had found out he had a few couchsurfers staying with him before they headed to northern Ethiopia. His place was conveniently situated within easy reach of transportation. He arranged a pickup for me from his home at four a.m.—apparently, it was standard practice. The transportation was a minibus, which drove around collecting people before driving like crazy to Beharadr. I had heard so much about those minibuses, and a few people had told me to avoid them. I understood why not only when I saw how the driver was driving, but also when I saw an overturned minibus on the side of the road. I took the risk because I wanted to cut my travel time to the border, as I knew it was going to be a long drive. My Japanese friends decided to meet me in Gonder the next day.

I spent the night in Beharadr, a town I had already visited before, and liked very much. After walking around by the lake,

Maskarm Haile

I had a quiet dinner and went to my hotel early to get ready for my early morning bus. I took yet another bus to Gonder the next day to meet up with my friends and head to the border town of Metema. When we arrived, it was in the heat of the afternoon. They told us that as the bus for Khartoum was only available in the morning, it would be better for us to stay on the Ethiopian side. The only accommodation was a shack like I had stayed in in Yabelo. It was 20 Birr or US $1, but at least it had an outdoor shower.

It was hot, and the flies were gigantic. We had the entire afternoon and evening to relax. We were all sweating profusely, and no amount of warm water satisfied my thirst. I decided to try Ethiopian beer out of desperation. I'm not a beer person, and to my surprise, it worked! The one cold drink available in the shop was beer; everything else was served warm, I guess.

There was nothing much to do in the hot, dusty town, so we tried walking up and down the street, surrounded by local kids. We went in and out of local bars to drink coffee and chat with people. If there was one thing I loved in that place, it was the local steam bread. The men baked the bread and there were long queues to buy it, but it was worth every minute of waiting for it.

The border crossing was easy since we had our visas. It was Ramadan, and we were told we might not find anything to eat on the way, and the bus ride might take a little more than eight hours. As I was sitting on the bus admiring the desert and the occasional goats I saw, I remembered our Sudanese family friends, the two Sudanese man who came to Ethiopia every year for their holidays. Later on, I understood they use to live in Riyadh, Saudi Arabia. But they were the first Sudanese people I had come across. They used to bring tins of Quality Street chocolates, and I got to choose which ones I wanted.

Abyssinian Nomad

Of course, I wanted them all—it was like Christmas in our house. It also meant unexpected family visits over the weekend, and they were by far my favorite guests. Sometimes my parents played some Sudanese music (they also went out partying quite a bit when the guests were around), and I remember how much they loved strong perfumes. My mother loved fragrances, and my dad even wore eau de toilette, but when our Sudanese friends came to visit, I would never know if I was smelling my mom's perfume or theirs. They filled my childhood with happy memories, and for me, Sudanese people meant kindness and joy.

It was a hot day and a long bus ride; we were told we would be in Khartoum after dark. The bus was full and every now and then I would chat with my fellow travelers. Suddenly, we saw a few men standing by the side of the road and waving for us to stop. I thought nothing of it—maybe they wanted to send something to Khartoum, or they just wanted to go to Khartoum. Anything was possible.

They were from the nearby mosque, and knowing people had been fasting all day and were still traveling at the time for the break of the fast in the evening, they invited strangers to eat with them. They welcomed the whole busload of people! As we got off the bus, women were told to go to one side and men were shown a different entrance. I asked one of the women if it was only for Muslims. Some of the people knew what to do, and some had already started to pray. Satomi and I hung out with the other ladies who weren't praying and just waited, not knowing what was taking place. I was touched as they went out of the way to feed us. We had barely crossed the border, and I was already experiencing the generosity of Sudanese people. After the prayers, it was a feast, and we all sat on the rugs on the floor. The food was placed in the middle, and we shared a meal as big happy family. I loved the way they made peanut butter, and eggplant salad.

Maskarm Haile

When we arrived in Khartoum, my host, Mohammed, was waiting for me. He had told me he would be happy to host me, but it was going to be at his office, not his parents' house. There was no way his parents would approve of women staying in their house while he was single. Understanding the culture, I was so grateful to Mohammed for going the extra mile to give me shelter.

Every day after Iftar, or for Iftar, the Ramadan meal after fasting the whole day, we met up with Mohammed and some of the couchsurfing community in Khartoum. They were fun, young, and different from past generations. Embracing world culture and sitting around with shisha, drinking tea, and eating dates and amazing Sudanese sweets, we laughed until our stomachs hurt. Then, at two in the morning Satomi, Akio, and I would walk back to our host slowly and quietly without waking anyone.

During the day, everything was so quiet we could hardly find anything open. So we stayed in, and we went out when it got a little cooler. On our first day, we decided to walk by the Nile while we were waiting for our friends to call after Iftar. We took a taxi, and it was evident the man was in a hurry to go home before the call to prayers. He dropped us by the river as we asked, then we paid and he left.

We walked for a while admiring the Nile (Abaye in Amharic) I had heard so much about it growing up. The Nile River is life for millions of people in Uganda, Ethiopia, Sudan and Egypt. Watching an Imax film about the Nile River in 2005 had even inspired me to learn more about the culture and lives of the people around the Nile. The Sudanese friends I had made over the years had given me an idea of how they go for a walk and tea after a hot day. I finally understood the Nile River brought cool air.

While walking, we ran into an old man who had just finished his prayer and was opening his lunch box to eat (Iftar).

He invited us to sit and eat with him, and he wouldn't take no for an answer. We shared his one small box of delicious food and chatted. He was a taxi driver, and his house was far away. After the meal, we walked with him to where he said there was a place for tea. It was just incredible to feel that connection; it was pure and profound in the way it happened.

As we sat down for tea, I realized my phone was missing. I'd had the phone in my hand when we left the house. That phone was a lifeline where I got my news and emails, and all my couchsurfing addresses were stored in it. I panicked. The old man calmly asked for my number and dialed it as we were talking and sure enough, someone answered. It turned out I had left my phone in the taxi, and the driver had been waiting for me to call. He told the driver where we were, and in a few minutes, he showed up with my phone.

I couldn't believe it. I remembered most people warning me about being robbed, but I had left my phone in the taxi, and the driver brought it to where I was. It was very touching. Yes, the cash I had kept with me to use in Sudan was missing when I got to Khartoum. I had no idea where I had lost it. Of course, I was disappointed. But Satomi lent me money until we arrived in Egypt and I could have ATM access again.

After a few days of bliss in Khartoum, we decided to head north. After all, our days in the country were limited. So, regretting we couldn't see more, we went to the bus stop to embark on the long journey to Port Sudan. While waiting for the bus, we started chatting with a Sudanese man we had just met. He said his name was Aarif and we all instantly fell in love with him; luckily, the feeling was mutual. Aarif was a symbol of goodness and kindness, a true Sudanese ambassador. We thought it was unfortunate we were leaving Khartoum when we met him; and we were frantically trying to figure out our bus route after Port Sudan to connect with the train.

Maskarm Haile

We also had to buy the train and ferry ticket while still at the bus station before leaving Khartoum. But as it was Ramadan, there were not many people in the office early in the morning to give us information. Those who were there could barely understand what we were talking about. It was understandable. Everyone went to bed at five in the morning and had to be at the office at seven. Even we were sleep deprived after being out until early morning chatting and drinking tea with our friends.

The problem was there was only a train twice a week, and we couldn't afford to miss the next one. If that happened, our visa would expire, and we would be in deep trouble in Sudan.

Understanding the urgency of the situation, Aarif went with us to figure it out. But no luck! When it was time for the bus to leave, he said he would sort everything for us and not to worry. We just needed to exchange our numbers.

So off we went on the bus to Port Sudan. As we had gone all the way there, we agreed the highlight of our trip would be diving in the Red Sea. I fantasized about lying on the beach and reading books in Port Sudan. It had been my dream since I was unable to get to Massawa, Eritrea, when my visa was refused twice. I thought Port Sudan would make up for it.

When we arrived and I saw the Red Sea in the distance, the long, excruciating bus ride with hundreds of checkpoints (each time we needed to get off and back on the bus in temperatures of over 40 degrees C) was forgotten. I was just so happy that I had made it. Looking at the turquoise water, I thought there was nothing that the beautiful, salty water couldn't soothe.

The town looked like a ghost town, but we thought it was because of the heat and Ramadan. We didn't find a host or any couchsurfers, so we went to the guesthouse that was recommended by the Lonely Planet Guidebook.

Abyssinian Nomad

In the evening, when the sun cooled off a little bit, and the shops and restaurants opened, we went for a walk by the water, ate some ice cream and found out about the diving trips. After all, they were the only reason we had come this far. When we arrived at the water, it was still quiet. In the distance, I saw people on a boat. Though they were on board and weren't expecting visitors; we invited ourselves.

I could see their surprise, but also their concern at us being on the boat. We didn't know, as single women, we weren't supposed to be on the boat with men. Nevertheless, the people on the boat were friendly, and we introduced ourselves. We explained what we were looking for. Both men looked at us with sad faces, as we had gone all the way to Port Sudan, and it was the off-season for diving. The boat we were on was usually used for privately hired diving trips of five to seven days, and it was expensive.

There was one more problem: we didn't have visas. We thought we would go for a day dive and leave for the train the next day. Feeling very disappointed, we just stood there chatting with the men. I found out that Felix, the Dutch guy I was talking to, had been living in Sudan for years and now because his family had packed up and left, and he too would be leaving Sudan soon. Hearing how the three of us, Satomi, Akio and me had met, he said we could go and stay in his empty house. Everything had been packed and was gone, but he still had a few mattresses lying in the house.

The next morning, we moved in with our backpacks. Still feeling a little upset, we went and visited the fish market, where they brought out the huge fish—their daily catch. The market was empty, but the fishermen were busy washing their catch of the day. All the colorful big fish I wanted to see in the water were displayed on the cutting boards, their beautiful colors still vibrant. We walked around and ate more ice cream while chatting with the Eritreans and Ethiopians working in the ice cream shops and restaurants.

Maskarm Haile

Aarif had been in touch with us every day, and he had managed to make a reservation for our train and ferry. All we had to do was take the night bus to connect to the train the next day. Simple! We got our bags ready, thanked Felix, and headed to the bus stop, only to find out we couldn't leave Port Sudan without an exit stamp from the authorities. What authorities? We hadn't needed a different visa when we came, but we needed an exit visa. We would have to wait until the next morning to get that stamp. By then we would have missed not only the bus but also the train and the boat. Our visa would expire! We were doomed. We did not want to get stuck in Port Sudan.

I called Felix to tell him what was going on, and he offered us his house while we sorted out our visas. None of us slept well that night. Going to a Sudanese jail was not the kind of thing we wanted to think about. Early in the morning when they opened the immigration office, we were there. As it was Ramadan, not many people were happy to work in the morning or show up on time. We were also told they closed the office early, so we had to sit and wait until someone decided to call us in. Once again, it was okay for the two Japanese to wander around Africa, but I was given lectures, advice, and some people even offered me their brothers and friends for marriage.

One woman suggested that as Sudanese men love Ethiopian women so much, she wouldn't have a problem finding me someone and marrying me off in a week. I just smiled and played along, as it was not the place for me to give my opinion. We went to a different office to repeat our story and fill out never-ending forms. Our papers were examined by various officers and stamped with caution. It seemed as if almost everyone in the office had to touch and stamp our passports. While it was all taking place, one woman actually understood how worried we were, and she tried to calm us and promised she would make sure we had our extension before the day ended. When finally, our extension visas were approved and we had paid, the officials discovered that they had run out of tourist visa stamps in their office.

Our hearts sank. An emergency meeting was called, and people were blaming each other for not ordering the visas from Khartoum. We just sat in a corner keeping our fingers crossed. Finally feeling proud and smiling from ear to ear, one of the officials came to us to tell us the good news. They were going to stamp our passports with resident visa stamps. *What, with a resident visa?*

I knew that the visa would get me out of Sudan but would get me into trouble somewhere else someday. But that was the least of my worries then. While our passports were being stamped, Mariam, the lady who had been super-friendly and promised to help us, invited us to go to her place for Iftar that evening. Of course, we accepted the offer and asked if we could also bring our host with us. When we arrived at her place, it was a feast. It was as if she had catered for ten more people. She had prepared every kind of local food, soups, and salads with dessert. We played with her children and cousins, but when she decided to take out all her colorful dresses, we had some fun playing dress-up in her bedroom away from the guys. The men, including her young son, were all in the living room, while we were in the bedroom trying on all the dresses. That morning, Mariam was in her office as an immigration officer, but later she was like a girl next door who was having fun with strangers trying on her dresses. We were all so grateful for the fantastic time we had. It had been a long day, and who could have known that our day with its bad visa scare would end on such a high note.

When we woke in the morning, we had our visas and a little time, so we decided to take it easy for the day. Our trip still needed a little coordination, and Aarif was helping us with that again. When my friends decided to stay home, I decided I was going to find a beautiful beach and swim. I was still obsessed with the idea of swimming, snorkeling, and diving in the Red Sea. After all, it was my birthday, and I deserved to celebrate my day by lying on the beach and swimming with the fish at least.

It was already hot, but I wasn't worried. I wore my bikini inside my clothes and covered my head because I couldn't walk around without my head cover. I walked to the beach where we met the guys that night, but I was looking for a beautiful private place, so I continued to walk.

Out of the corner of my eye, I saw a group of men, some sitting and some standing. I could feel them staring at me from afar. I was a little worried—if I could feel them looking at me like that, what would they do when I got closer? But there was nowhere else to go, so I continued walking. When I got closer, one of them seemed to be indicating to someone to come to him. I thought there might be someone else behind me, and I turned to look. No one was there.

I was a little annoyed when I realized I was the one he had been signaling with his fingers. I almost ignored him, but he jumped up and walked towards me, and all the other men (about ten to twelve of them) walked behind him. Before I knew it, I was surrounded by them, all looking at me.

The guessing games started, and some of them said I was Ethiopian and the others Eritrean. I could see the main guy was angry because he felt disrespected in front of his friends, and I was feeling disrespected by the way he'd tried to call me. I wondered who he thought he was to call me like that and say that I wasn't dressed appropriately. He suddenly asked for my passport. More questions flooded through my mind. Why would he want my passport? Who was he? The men were wearing shirts, but nothing about them looked like police or immigration officers. I almost asked for proof of his identity.

Abyssinian Nomad

Everyone was watching, and he seemed to think that I was in Sudan illegally to earn some income like most Ethiopian and Eritreans do to survive. Judging by the way he looked at me, he wanted me to beg or ask for mercy. The others seemed to be supporting him.

The truth was I didn't have my passport or any proof of identity with me. I told them I was out for a swim, and my passport was at a friend's home. I was still not sure why I needed to show him my passport. They all went quiet for a moment, and the guys who understood were shocked by what I said. They translated for their friends and almost burst out laughing, but I saw they were afraid of offending the man who was arguing with me. He said women are not allowed to swim in the sea and that I needed to follow him to the police station. I tried to explain that I had a passport and even an extended visa. He seemed to think that I needed to pay for being disrespectful and wanting to swim. I realized things were getting serious; I was surrounded by men walking to the police station. A fearful thought came to my mind. If he put me in jail, no one would know where I was.

I tried phoning Felix to ask him to bring my passport, but he didn't answer. Then I remembered I had Mariam's number, so I called her. By then we were almost at the police station, and the man didn't want to talk to Mariam. In his eyes, I was a criminal because I talked back to a man.

Understanding the seriousness of the situation, I calmed down, but the only person who could save me was Mariam at the end of the phone. He refused to talk to her again, but one of his friends took the phone and spoke to her. Suddenly, it was clear that I was a Canadian and my visa was in order. My phone was going back and forth among the men, who were still asking her questions about me. In the meantime, I was taken inside a room where an older man in uniform sat. I was told to sit, and the man gave a lengthy explanation in Arabic. I didn't understand a word of it, but I knew he was trying to find a reason why I'd been brought in.

When the older man turned to look at me, Mariam was still on the phone, and I asked him to speak to her if he had doubts about my passport and visa. He took the phone. When he hung up, he was very compassionate and almost embarrassed by how the younger man had treated me. He tried to explain that they have lots of illegal people in the country, but most importantly, he said they didn't like it when a woman was strong and talked back. He said he was going to do something special for me.

I had no idea what that meant, but I waited. All I wanted was not to be in a Sudanese jail, and it looked like I was saved by Mariam and the older man. He called two police officers and asked them to escort me to the beach, and said I could go into the water for five minutes, fully clothed. I was grateful for his gesture and kindness. But my initial idea of getting into a bikini, sunbathing, and floating in the salty ocean wasn't going to happen. I couldn't wait to reunite with my traveling buddies and our host. I was ready to leave Port Sudan.

Later that day, my friends surprised me with a birthday cake and a beautiful photo album they had made of our travels. We sat around on the floor and ate cake while talking about how close we were to the end of our journey. I had no idea where I was going to be for my next birthday, but I knew it would be very, very different. So much had happened. It touched my heart that my friends went out of their way to print some pictures and make an album for me. It had been an incredible gift to be able to travel with them. Akio had become like a husband to both of us; just his presence was protection from unwanted attention. It had been lots of fun.

The next day we decided to go back to Khartoum via Kassala. It was one of the places we had wanted to go but hadn't yet because of having to get our visas, but now that we had sorted out the visas, we also wanted to spend some time with Aarif, who had become like family to us. He called us every day and made sure everything was going well with us. We didn't even know him, but he made sure our train and boat were booked while we were in Port Sudan, and he had canceled everything for us when we missed our bus. I wondered how Aarif could give so much to complete strangers that he had known for less than an hour.

When we arrived in Kassala, for the first time I was grateful we missed our bus, and we got our extended visa. Almost every Sudanese man or women I had met in the past never stopped talking about Kassala and Omdurman. Once we got to Kassala, I saw why. Kassala was believed to be a sacred place for Sudanese honeymooners. The Taka Mountains were a backdrop for a holy well that was said to enhance fertility. Eritrea was just over the mountains. The market was big and vibrant. We went up and down the hill playing like kids as the sun set, changing the color of the stones around us. We drank tea with the locals and Eritreans, who were trying to figure me out.

When we arrived in Khartoum, it was like we had gone back home. I didn't know how a place where we had spent so little time could feel so much like home. Seeing Aarif at the bus station was like having a family reunion. We were connected to him way before we really knew him. Every time he called, he made sure he talked to each of us. When I told him I had been taken to the police station, he was very disappointed by how women were treated in Sudan. He had said we were going to stay at his apartment, and we were all happy. We also couldn't wait to introduce him to our couchsurfing family in Khartoum.

Aarif opened his house and his heart to us. He made sure we saw all the places we had missed before because we had left early. We went to the biggest camel market in Omdurman, where a wealthy octogenarian camel merchant offered to marry me. He was willing to pay thirteen camels to my father and two to me. We all laughed, but he was serious.

The day we took Aarif to the couchsurfing family was one of the happiest days for all of us. We had no idea the couchsurfing family had occupied so much space in all our hearts. It was indeed a joyous moment seeing them again, and we were proud to introduce another genuinely fantastic human being we had accidentally found in Sudan. We made him a couchsurfer too.

The last few days we spent with Aarif were by far the most precious time I had spent in Sudan. We engaged in amazing conversations full of openness, filled with hopes and dreams, desires and genuine kindness. In that small apartment, we all cooked together and talked until the wee hours. As if all that wasn't enough, Aarif and I found out we had one common interest—India! He, too, had lived in India, and he felt connected to the place and the people. He was about to finish the book, *Shantaram*. Later, he ended up giving it to me to read.

At last it was time to say goodbye to our "friend-families" and embark on the long journey from Khartoum to Wadi Halfa.

Chapter 25: Wait, Did I Just...

"The afterlife was incredibly important to the Egyptians. They believed that by preserving a dead person's body – which they did through the process of mummification – their soul would live on in the afterlife forever."
~ 10 facts about Ancient Egypt

AFTER THE LONG, DUSTY, HOT, train ride on the most uncomfortable seats, I was happy to be on the ferry. I had opted for the first-class sleeper after hearing all the stories about it on the train, while my friends had chosen a general cabin to sit in and sleep on the floor. I also wanted a little time on my own to reflect on my trip. I could hardly believe I had made it that far.

Technically, I was in Egypt. *"I am here!"* I said to myself. My impossible dream had come true! I had been so focused on crossing the next border that I hadn't had time to think about what would happen next. And then the sad reality hit home again: my mother was not there anymore to share my moments. Apart from my mom and a few others, not many people understood the depth of my desire to fulfill my dream.

So, it was sad I couldn't share my news with her, but I promised to write an email to everyone who had been with me in spirit, on my journey.

As I was sitting on the ferry watching the sunset, I felt that the heavens were celebrating with me. The sky had exploded into colors of orange and red, and my body shook with excitement and gratitude. I had made it, I was in Egypt, and my dream had come true. Who would have thought that a girl from Ethiopia could not only dream, but also have her dreams come true?

There was a sense within me that I had arrived, not only physically but metaphorically. The journey had been a long, challenging one. I had experienced love, loss, fear, sadness, and feeling lost, but right at that moment, though I was physically tired, I felt alive! I felt light, as if I had given birth to something. The nine-month journey had taken everything out of me, but I felt as though a new me had emerged from it all. I was not the same person; I could never be the same. I could not go back to who I had been. When I started my journey, I was convinced if Africa didn't kill me, it would heal me.

But now, not only was I still alive, I felt deeply transformed. Mother Africa had come to my rescue. Losing everything I thought I knew, wanted, and needed had given a deeper meaning to my life, and I had come out stronger on the other side. Though I wasn't able to articulate it at that time, I was feeling a new depth and strength of knowingness within me. I was walking out of my labyrinth with my lesson to carry with me through my life. My tears streamed under my big sunglasses, but they were happy tears; they were tears of gratitude! Yes, I wished my mother was still alive, but I knew she was cheering me on from above. For the last year or so, I had been so focused on the journey that I had no idea what I wanted or would be doing at the end of it. That I was in Egypt and still alive meant that I would need a plan for my future.

Abyssinian Nomad

About four hours after our departure in Wadi Halfa, we were treated with a glimpse of Abu Simbel, illuminated against the darkness of the night. We knew then; we had to do the trek back by road the next day to see the temples.

Egypt was everything I'd expected and wished for, and simultaneously everything I hadn't expected and thus never wished for. As soon as we arrived at the port in Aswan, I witnessed a human stampede as people rushed to get their luggage out of the ferry. It was terrifying to watch, but that wasn't all—it was the same for the taxis and buses. Egyptians never take no for an answer! The four of us, with our new Dutch friend, Mark, decided to go to the same hotel by the Nile, sharing rooms as only travelers do. The only calm thing we did that I remember was dropping our backpacks in our rooms and jumping into the pool as the sun was setting. Watching the traditional felucca and cruise ships floating on the Nile River from the hotel pool was just surreal.

I was so grateful to those hard-core Japanese travelers and friends I'd met in a very unusual place, and with whom I had traveled so far. It was almost time for us to be going our separate ways, but I knew they were my gift from above.

Akio had tried to protect us. He was the young but big brother when we needed him, and our sometimes pretend-husband to chase away the unwelcome attention from men who pestered Satomi and me. I had grown fond of my two Japanese friends. Yes, sometimes we didn't see things eye to eye, but I loved how they had the courage and desire to see and to connect with people. We shared one thing: we all loved meeting people, and our driving force was our passion for people.

After the sunset, we ventured to the popular night bazar filled with colorful spices, souvenirs and aggressive shopkeepers who'll do anything to get your business. But it being my first night and just off the boat, I was too excited and happy to be bothered by over-friendliness.

Maskarm Haile

After we got back to our hotel that night we were on a mission: Booking our organised tour to Abu Simba for the next day. The buses travel in convoy since there was recently an attack in the area. We opted for the 11 a.m. bus and ebressed the 290 km journey in hot dry sun. But when we reached and entered the temple, it was worth every penny and the time and energy we had to spend to trek back almost to the Sudanese border once again.

The two Temples of Abu Simbel, with their unique style, are considered to be the masterpieces of ancient Egypt. They were built to commemorate the region of Ramses II, the greatest Pharaoh and his wife Nefertari. The amazing size of the temples is jaw-dropping and I wondered how they were able to move them from the original place to avoid the flood. Inside the twin Temples there are preserved paintings, statues, and chambers. We walked around feeling small and in awe among the massive structures. There is no easy way to express the feeling one gets walking around a historical, ancient monument that stands bigger, and stronger than us as humans.

After we went back to Aswan for a night, the next day I headed to Luxor, planning to reconnect with my friends in Cairo later in the week. I stayed in a backpackers' hostel where the owner happen to be a couchsurfer who helped me choose a day trip to Valley of the Kings, Queen Hatshepsut Temple, and Luxor and Karnak temples. The small town located on the bank of the Nile is filled with the spirit of the mighty ancient civilization. Luxor used to be known as Thebes to the outside world, and it is like an open-air museum, with ancient wonders to be found in every corner. It's amazing to witness what Egyptian craftsmen were able to accomplish thousands of years ago. It didn't feel right to run around the temples, trying to grasp the magnitude of the history and the sight of the grand structures in just the 8-10 hours our tour provided. The temple has massive stone statues, and towering pillars that make it unique. Most of all, the temple is lit up by series of lights, which make it stand out in the centre of the city. Though it was hard to compare or chose, I spent more time at the incredible temple of Karnak. The site is one of the largest religious structure ever built, and so important to ancient Egyptians that numerous pharos continued to add chapels, obelisks, statues and chambers over the centuries. It was breath-taking to say the least.

I loved Luxor. There were people everywhere in the colorful night markets. By day it was a mission to see the endless historical sights and museums. The Egyptians are experts in herding people. The queues to most places were insanely long, with tourists from all over the world. Egyptians also tend to see money when they see tourists, and when they see women tourists, they see sex and money. The intensity was just too much; I didn't have any place or experience I could compare it to.

The history was unbelievable: everything you saw or touched had a story, everything was valued and appreciated. But for the first time, I found myself wishing I was traveling with a male partner more often. My visit as a solo traveler turned into a nightmare overnight. It was almost too hard to handle it; I converted to a stalker looking for other single travelers, preferably men. Saying that my husband was in Canada didn't work there. The men were aggressive and downright rude at times. I was the Nubian, and they were the Egyptians. They had stories to tell me but always ended by asking me to have sex or just touching my face or body. In all my travels, it was the first time I had been harassed like that. I almost begged other tourists to let me walk with them, especially in the archaeological sites, since the sites are big and isolated and I didn't want men following me.

I took a train to Cairo and reunited with Satomi and Akio, at the big Iftar meal in Cairo with over twenty couchsurfers.

Maskarm Haile

Both locals and travelers equally represented. It was nice to see familiar face comforting to meet locals who were not there to sell you something or ask for sex.

Satomi was flying out of Cairo, but Akio was staying a few more weeks to travel. I later ran into him in the middle of Dahab before he flew out.

I had been in touch with Asim, a couchsurfer, having sent a request a few months earlier. We'd been exchanging emails, but my arrival had taken way too long. So, when I sent him an email to say I was in the country, he was devastated at not being able to host me anymore because he had moved back to his parents' house to save some money for his next travel. But he had been following my journey and we'd been chatting for a while, so he wanted to help me. He asked one of his young cousins who was a university student to host me in his two-bedroom apartment. I graciously accepted the offer and thanked his cousin. I even thought maybe he too would become a couchsurfer after all. It was Ramadan, and after I went to the apartment with them, dropped my backpack, and took a shower, we all went out for Iftar.

The couchsurfers had organized to meet in a friendly restaurant. It was one of the biggest couchsurfer dinners I had been to since South Africa, and I was thrilled. There were local people and couchsurfers from around the world. I felt at home. Oh, the food! I was in heaven. After a long dinner, we moved to a hookah bar where we drank tea while some of them smoked and swapped travel stories until the early morning. Asim was happy. I was in good hands with his cousin, and I was as comfortable as I could be with strangers. My head spun from everything—things I had seen, stories I had heard—and I felt I was in my element. I went back home with the cousin, and Asim went back to his parents' house.

When I got to the cousin's house, he said there were rules in the house like the bathroom door must be open when showering, and the bedroom door must remain unlocked. What he said was so bizarre that I thought he was joking and I didn't really take him seriously. After all, Asim was there, and he had hosted numbers of couchsurfers before me. But when we got back, something within me said to lock my bedroom door. It was the first time I had had such a feeling. I had surfed many couches, and most of the time there wasn't even a door to lock. I had shared rooms with strangers, and it had never been an issue for me. But that day, through my exhaustion, the voice inside my head was loud and clear. I almost regretted what I was hearing, but my intuition was not negotiable. All the time I had been traveling alone, my only weapon was my intuition. I had determined not to fight, argue with, nor doubt my inner voice. There was no being in the middle when it came to trusting people.

I learned years ago, early on in my travels, that I needed to trust myself and my dreams to take me where I needed to be. And ever since, I had witnessed what I call my intuition getting bigger and louder within me. I had also learned when I broke my promises, got entangled in my thoughts, or didn't listen to it, there was a price to pay.

So far, payment for not trusting myself had been mostly material, maybe being overcharged, losing stuff, or missing my bus—that kind of thing. But that night it was about self-preservation. I was tired, and I'd had a fantastic evening with a total stranger, but I didn't want to fight my intuition.

Almost half-asleep, I got out of my bed and locked the bedroom door. I didn't know if the cousin had come and found out the door was locked or if he had heard me lock it. I didn't remember anything; I slept like a baby. But when I woke up in the morning, I knew something wasn't quite okay, and I didn't want to be there anymore. I slowly opened the door, took a quick shower, and got ready. As I felt sorry about leaving without telling my friend Asim first, I left my backpack in the apartment and went out. I was supposed to see Asim that evening, and there was another couchsurfers' gathering for Iftar. After hanging out at the museum in town, I decided to go to a backpacker hostel in the city and ask if they had a place for me. The people there were friendly, and I saw a couchsurfer I had met at the dinner the previous day. She confirmed the place was good, and safe for women. I booked myself a bed.

When I met up with Asim, I could see how distressed he was feeling. He had something to tell me but couldn't make himself say it, and I felt the same. He had been so helpful and kind to me; how could I tell him I didn't feel safe staying with his cousin? Finally, Asim turned to me and said his cousin couldn't host me any longer, but I could only collect my backpack when he got back at three a.m. I was relieved, but the idea of being in a taxi at three a.m. was terrifying. Unfortunately, Asim had to go home for Iftar with his family and wouldn't be able to go out later that night. Also, his cousin had said if I didn't take my backpack that night, he wouldn't be around the following day. I knew he was angry when I'd seen him that the morning, and suddenly it all made sense.

I needed to figure out something soon; there was no way I could take a taxi on my own at three a.m. and also trust Asim's cousin to show up at his apartment. Asim felt bad. I thanked him and told him it would be okay. In the evening, when we gathered for Iftar, I approached one of the couchsurfer ambassadors. I was also a couchsurfer roving ambassador, but what I wanted to discuss had nothing to do with couchsurfing. Asim's cousin was not a couchsurfer, and I knew that before I went to his home. But my only option was to turn to couchsurfers to help me. The ambassador was very thoughtful and kind. He both reassured me and went with me to get my backpack. It was a very awkward situation to be in at three a.m. I wasn't sure if Asim's cousin would be aggressive or nice about the whole thing, but I told my couchsurfing friend to wait for me outside and went in on my own. I still wanted to respect my host's space, so I didn't want to take a stranger to his apartment. When he opened the door, I just said hello from afar, though usually I hug my hosts. I thanked him for hosting me the previous night, walked in and picked up my backpack and left. My heart was beating so fast, but I kept my eyes on him. I realized he couldn't even look at me. He just said sorry, he was busy.

I moved to a hostel in downtown Cairo, feeling a little shaken by what had happened, but also so grateful I'd listened to my intuition. I'd learned a lesson I will never forget. But it was also hard to not to think about what could have happened, and not to doubt myself with wondering, *did I miss a red flag?*

Anyone who knows me knows that I love books, and I wasn't going to pass on the opportunity to visit the Bibliotheca Alexandrina in Alexandria, which opened in October 2002 to reclaim the mantle of its ancient namesake. It was not only an extraordinarily beautiful building, but also a vast complex where arts, history, philosophy, and science come together. I took the train to Alexandria and joined a tour that took us into the eleven-story building for a one-hour tour with detailed explanations. The library's granite exterior walls are carved with letters, pictograms, hieroglyphs, and symbols from more than 120 different human scripts. Walking into the reading room that could easily accommodate eight million books and more than two thousand readers at a time, was, by itself truly overwhelming, in a good way. I wouldn't be exaggerating if I say, being in the library was one of my highlights traveling in Africa.

After spending my entire day at the library, I went out for a long walk by the beach in the evening. I was not feeling comfortable walking alone anymore—Egypt had traumatized me in a way I hadn't expected. I was used to slipping in and out of countries, but being called out to and touched had made me a fearful, angry traveler. At the same time, I loved everything else I saw, the history, culture, food, and some of the locals. It was just a weird contradiction what I was feeling.

A child approached me while I was walking on the beach and I wasn't super-friendly. I was paranoid and overly cautious. It was almost time for Iftar, and I knew people would flock to the beach after breaking fast and it wouldn't be quite so quiet anymore. But the boy wouldn't stop following me and smiling, almost waiting to reach out and touch me. After some time, I couldn't resist, and I stopped and asked him his name. He had a beautiful, beaming smile, and he said, "Nasser." Still walking with me, he started to hold my hand. I wondered where his family was and why was he alone running around on the beach. He didn't speak much English, but he seemed to understand when I said, "Your parents, mamma, and father." He pointed to the direction I had walked earlier, but as we had walked for a while, I thought his parents must be worried if they've found out their son has wandered off out of sight.

I told him to go back, but he wouldn't leave and kept holding my hand. He didn't ask me for anything, so I suggested we walk back the same way, and I would be able to drop him at his parents. When we arrived, I realized his father was getting ready for his night business of selling tea and snacks by the side of the road, and they were about to break their fast. The boy's older brother was helping his dad. The boy wouldn't let my go of my hand, and as I got closer and closer and the father and son welcomed me as if I was their guest they had been waiting for. The older brother spoke a little more English, and the father was happy to see me. They invited me to the table; the kids were quick to bring an extra chair for me so that I could eat with them. They wouldn't take no for an answer, and the father apologized for not have something special for me.

Abyssinian Nomad

Little did he know how special that moment was for me, once again being invited to a complete stranger's house and life. There was no deep conversation or swapping of stories, but enough love and trust poured from them to make me feel safe again. It was a sort of confirmation to me; there might be some sick people out there, but not everyone was a danger to me, and I was on the right track.

After dinner, I sat and drank tea, feeling the salty air on my face and hair. Clutching the tiny stranger's hands, surrounded by a father with his two sons, was a precious moment. They had no idea how they'd restored my trust in humanity or Egyptian men. I gave each one of them a long hug, feeling I was leaving my own family; I almost had tears in my eyes as I walked away.

Once in Cairo, I kept busy doing all the things tourists do. I have to say Cairo is not for the faint-hearted. The dirty streets can be unbearably hot and chaotic. But I loved the city! Just walking on the street and the open market and being pushed and pulled by vendors required strong survival skills. The one thing I could never master was crossing the street. No one stops their car to let pedestrians pass. I took to standing on the sides of the roads, waiting for those pedestrians to take the first step so that I could follow them.

I took my time when I visited the Museum of Cairo. The place is filled with antique Egyptian artifacts, more than 120,000 items dating back to ancient times. It is probably one of the most fascinating museums I have ever visited in the world. I was glad I was on my own and could linger as long as I wanted, because it was hard for me to leave that place.

Giza—no picture or video can transmit the great energy and power of the pyramids that I saw and felt. It is not possible to express what it was like to be there. I was totally in awe of the pyramids. Just the sheer sense of being there was overwhelming and raised so many questions for me. I couldn't wrap my head around the size and magnificence of the pyramids, or why and how they were built.

My experience was, however, marred by having to deal with an overzealous guide. Being a female solo traveler didn't help when I had to negotiate the payment for the camel ride or deal with the guide who kept insisting he wanted to sit with me on the camel even though I had said from the beginning that he should be on his own camel, and that I didn't want to sit with anyone. Sadly, having to fend off the guide and constantly argue with him took away so much from my experience.

A Sudanese man I met at the hostel told me he wanted to introduce me to his Ethiopian friend, so he called the woman and gave me the phone. I had no idea what I was supposed to do or say, and I'm sure she had no idea what was going on either. I apologized for what was happening and introduced myself. I heard her hesitation, and there was an awkward pause. I just said it was lovely talking to her and asked if she wanted me to pass the phone back to the Sudanese man. But she asked where I was staying and how long I was going to be around. I told her, and she said that Friday was her day off and she would call me. I gave her my number and passed the phone. But I didn't know if that meant we would meet or if she would just call me and talk; I had no idea. Usually, I want to know everything if I am planning my day, but I told myself, for all I knew she might not even call me. So, I didn't take the call that seriously.

On Thursday night, the start of the weekend, I was out with some couchsurfers horseback riding in the middle of the night to the pyramids. It had been a long time since I had been on the back of a horse, and certainly never at night. It was one of the most challenging things I had done since my white-water rafting in Uganda. It was exhilarating to feel the power of the horse I was riding, in the midst of the pyramids under the moonlit, starry night sky. It was cold in the desert, but being in the open with the stars and the moon was priceless. It's safe to say I didn't make it to my hostel until six in the morning. And I had forgotten entirely about the tentative phone call planned for Friday. Before I had even gotten out of my bed, the woman was already at my hostel and was calling me. I answered my phone, surprised she had called, but when she told me she was outside, I jumped out of bed, not knowing what the plan was, and I went out to say hello.

I apologized profusely for the way I looked. My hair was full of sand and I was half-asleep. I explained about my night. The next thing she said surprised me. She had come to take me to her house. Talk about being unprepared, but she said I could sleep at her house and she would make coffee for us and introduce me to her friend. I had no idea who she was and what she was doing in Egypt. And it was too early for me to even think of a conversation. But how could I say no to Ethiopian coffee and a new friend?

I took a quick shower. There was no time to wash my hair since her friend was waiting for us. Feeling like I had a hangover without having had any alcohol, I followed her, a complete stranger, to a taxi stand and I hopped in a taxi without even knowing where I was going. I tried to stay awake and make conversation. She told me she worked for an Egyptian family and she and her friend rent an apartment only for their days off, so they could cook, wash and have their privacy at least once a week or so. She happened to have a day off. Though she wasn't sure about me, she felt responsible to come and meet me just because I am Ethiopian. She said we needed to help each other and wanted to make sure I wouldn't get in trouble as most newcomers do.

It was only then I realized that I hadn't even told her I was just a traveler passing through Egypt. Her kindness touched my heart, and I was just happy to have met her and to spend time with her. When we got to her home, she told me to have a nap, and when I woke up she had already cooked food—she had made Injera—and I could smell the Ethiopian coffee she was roasting. Her friend was as welcoming as she was. Now that I had slept a little bit I could think clearly and wondered what they must have thought of my life. It was clear we had very different lives and probably not much in common, but for the moment we were happy in each other's company, laughing, sharing, and cherishing the moment.

They even decided my hair needed a good wash and treatment because there was still sand in it from the night before. It felt like we came from two different worlds; they could never understand why I was on the back of a horse eating dust in the middle of the night with a bunch of people I barely knew. I showed them some pictures, and they only laughed. Eating Injera and drinking Ethiopian coffee helped us to bring our two different worlds together. It was an unexpectedly beautiful connection, as pure as it could be. I was so grateful for the man who connected us.

Though it had been a pain hiring a camel and guide at Giza, I spent the day climbing up and down pyramids on a hot sunny day. I was awed by what I saw; the truth was ever since I arrived in Egypt, I had been fascinated every day. And I appreciated the way the Egyptians kept their history and shared it with the world. I was grateful to be able to see a living museum and not just read about it or watch it on TV.

By the time I was ready to leave, I was tired and I needed a well-deserved holiday for a few days by the ocean. I also had to think about my future. In one of the couchsurfing Iftar dinners, I had met a Canadian couple who were traveling in the Middle East; they had just crossed the border from Jordan, and we were swapping travel stories. Like everyone else, they had asked me what was next. The answer was still that I didn't know! The truth was I hadn't gone that far in my mind yet. I gave them information on Sudan, in case they wanted to continue traveling into the rest of Africa, and we ended up exchanging books. They gave me their Middle East Lonely Planet Guidebook. I jokingly said that was dangerous for me, but I took the guidebook anyway and made sure to put it deep in my backpack, so I didn't even think about it.

I couldn't have asked for a better place to end my nine-month journey in Africa than Dahab. Dahab, the fishing village by the Red Sea, was discovered by hippies and turned into a quiet diving village. It was surrounded by the Sinai Desert, friendly Bedouins, a glowing moon and stars at night, and of course the colorful, magical Red Sea filled with life.

There was something about the place that instantly calmed my spirit. As if my work was done, and it was time to slow down. No bus ticket to buy, museum to visit, or border to cross.

I checked into a reasonable hotel on the beach, feeling I had come a long way and deserved some quiet time to reflect about my journey and enjoy a little holiday before whatever I decided to do next.

I rented snorkeling equipment for three days. *Finally I can wear my bikini and get into the Red Sea without worrying about being thrown into jail*, I thought. But that dream was very short-lived because being a solo woman traveler, I attracted unwanted attention from the young Egyptian boys who followed me into the water and almost drowned me, when they started throwing themselves on me. I was very disappointed until I joined a group of people for afternoon and evening diving and snorkeling. Finally, one of my dreams had been realized, and I couldn't have been happier.

Though I made friends and went out for dinner, I was in a hurry to come back and sit by the water. The heat of the day was replaced with the desert wind at night, which made it a little chilly. Wearing my wraparound scarf and covering myself with a towel, I just sat there listening to the water. And then, it just happened. I wasn't planning it like that. My plan had been in the next day or so, I'd take out my journal, sit on my balcony and reflect on my journey and write about my experience. But no, it was like I was watching a movie. It all unfolded right in front of me under the glowing moon in a Sani desert.

I replayed almost everything, including the experiences I'd thought were nothing and shrugged off. I laughed, cried, giggled, and sometimes wondered how I'd survived. The generosity of strangers I'd encountered warmed my heart all over again. Right there and then I knew something had changed, something had shifted within me. The tears flooding my face weren't sad tears anymore; the feeling of hopelessness and distress was gone, and a new excitement was arising within me.

Even when I told myself I didn't know what I was going to do next, there was nothing that could dim my rising enthusiasm about my new life.

That night as I was falling asleep, emotionally charged, but physically tired, I felt a warm sensation all over my body and a presence around me. In my dream, I saw my mother covering me with a blanket, as if she was tucking me in to sleep.

I decided it was time to find answers to the questions everyone had been asking me. Questions like:

"What is next for you?"

"Where are you going to be living?"

"Are you going to get married?"

"What will you be doing next?"

"Does this mean you will stop traveling?"

I, too, needed to find the answers for myself. Until then, it had been easy: I was traveling from Cape to Cairo, and no one had been interested in what I would do afterward because

Abyssinian Nomad

Cape to Cairo sounded like such a long journey. But being in Egypt and near the end of my journey, my lack of answers was making some friends and family uncomfortable.

On my fourth day, I decided to take out that Middle East Lonely Planet Guidebook from my backpack and transfer it into my daypack to accompany me to the beach knowing that if I started reading it, I would be crossing yet another border to Jordan. But before that, not knowing that it would be the last time, I entered the ocean once again for a nice refreshing swim, and on my way out I stood half in, half out of the water in the scorching sun, and I nodded my thanks for Africa.

Dankie Africa - for your beauty—the mountains, dessert, oceans, wildlife, flowers— everything in nature that healed my soul, was a feast to my eyes, and blew my mind.

Merci - for every experience and the life lessons you offered in my nine-months journey.

Asante Sana - For every human connection I was blessed with, connections that were meant for a reason, a season or a lifetime.

Amesegnalehu - for my rich and diverse heritage.

Abrigado - for the transformation that took place in my life, and the growth that came from every experience.

And most of all, Shukraan for the wisdom of Love, accepting, kindness, compassion

"Where you end up isn't the most important thing.
It's the road you take to get there.
The road you take is what you will look back on and call your life."
~ Tim Wiley

Acknowledgments

Dad - It's impossible to thank you adequately for everything you have done. Though you didn't bring me into this world, you have given me everything I needed to live my own life. Thank you for raising me, and instilling traditional values, and showing me how life is better when a man and woman are best friends and partners rather than a traditional husband and wife.

My Sisters - I thank you for allowing me to be me and to carve my own path. Thank you for shared memories and life lessons. Though I am not always around, and we don't get to do things sisters usually do, I'm grateful for your presence in my life. I could not have asked for better sisters.

My Grandparents - Thank you for loving me unconditionally when I needed to be loved and know I was loved.

Senait Worku (Antica Family) - Your generosity, love, and support are beyond words. I cherish every experience and the time that we share together, because they are enriching, effortless, and real. I am eternally grateful for having you all in my life.

Yonas Zegeye - Thank you for your random acts of kindness. Your generosity has helped me to bring the book you are holding to the world. The world is better and more beautiful because there are people like you in it.

Israel Dessalegne - I know that before anyone else, including me, you had a vision for this book and held that vision for nine years without giving up—even when I was so far from fulfilling it. Thank you for trusting my dream to travel, for your constant support. Most of all, my Cape to Cairo trip wouldn't have happened at the time it did, if it wasn't your trust in my dream and your convincing my mother to give me her blessing. You are the champion of this book. I hope I have made you proud.

Baba Berhane & Zaid Beyene - Thank you for adopting me into your family, for your constant reminders of what I'm able to do, and for the stories you shared. You have been my greatest fans who believed in the need to share my story with the world.

Nebeyu Shone - I met you on my epic Cape to Cairo journey and you have been pushing and encouraging me to write this book; I hope it makes you proud. Thank you for believing I had something to say!

Almaz Gebru - My deepest gratitude for the beautiful memories you created for me and my mother in South Africa and for your continued support and encouragement for me to share my story.

Megbar Ayalew - Not only do you create and hold space for me when I need it, you allow and encourage me to shine my light to others. How very fortunate I am to have your love, support, belief, and friendship. Thank you!

Nahusenay Girma - I always believed when someone pushes you from your comfort zone and is brutally honest, it means that person cares and believes in you. You have been that person. It was your voice that brought me back to life when I had my breakdown over this book. I can't thank you enough.

Donna Barker - You are the miracle woman, the incredible midwife of this book. Thank you for allowing me to fully embark on the writing journey and for picking up my phone calls, and answering my emails when I panicked. You put me right back on my path.

Erasmus Morah - Thank you for seeing me, and for witnessing my journey from the day my mom brought us together. I know the journey wasn't fun sometimes when I was feeling lost and confused, but thank you for sticking it out with me and never giving up.

Most of the first draft of the book was written at **Marion's family cottage** in **Mont-Laurier.** I am profoundly grateful for hosting and adopting me into the family for most of the writing process. I hope finally seeing the book makes you proud.

Lynne Marion - Twin soul, I don't know where to start to thank you. Your love, support, friendship, and presence in my life are a huge gift. Thank you for inspiring me, for enriching my life, and most of all for believing in me and witnessing my journey.

Aude - What can I say? Your gentle, loving, caring spirit, and your love and support over the years has been so incredible. I can't believe you survived my endless venting about my book. Seeing you and eating Chouquette every week was the best therapy ever. Thank you!

Minou the Cat - Minou slept on my lap, pushing my laptop away every night and day for about two months when I sat to write. She was my great companion who reminded me to breathe, smile, and just love unconditionally while I was in the maddest of my stress to finish this book. Thank you, and I love you, Minou!

Sandra Baker - You are my gift from above(Yvette). You believed in my story from the beginning, kept telling me I have a unique voice (Though I didn't believe you for a long time.), and labored to mold the manuscript to a readable form. Not only that, you asked me to dig deeper. The book is better because of you.

Mary Amato - I can never thank you enough for awakening my consciousness to my soul's higher purpose in life. My life is supremely richer because of your teaching.

Allison - Thank you for designing my website and book cover, and for your understanding of my story and easily capturing it in your work.

Piergiorgio Traversin - You captured my free spirit with your drawing in Argentia, who knew it will be on my book eight years later. Thank you for sharing your beautiful gift.

Jana, **Stephany**, **Charlotte**, **Dana**, - Without your editing, suggestions and encouragement this book wouldn't have reached this point. Thank you for your meticulous work.

Dr. Yohannes Woldeamuel - Thank you for answering my email and allowing me to quote you in the book.

Jashu - Our paths first crossed in that tiny village in Africa, and you have been a great friend and soul-searching partner. You that keep inspiring me and reminding me I have so much to give. Thank you for your unconditional love and support.

Dr. Bogale and his team at **Noble Higher Clinic** - I am sorry I never got a chance to thank you personally after leaving the hospital. I can't thank you enough for the level of care and understanding you provided to my mother and our family. You have a difficult job, but thank you for choosing to be kind and compassionate.

My mom's friends and clinic staff at UN Addis - We practically grew up under your watch. You all came together to help us, the kids, as your own. I remember you in more ways than I ever have given you credit for. Thank you for celebrating my birthdays, graduation, and for being there at the worst time of my life—losing my mother. This book is for you as much as it is for my mother.

Virginia - Thank you for being willing to chat with me to share your wisdom about the world of publishing which lead us to do this final project together. Thank you for making the book look fabulous with your magic.

To all listed here, and to many who are not, this acknowledgement would be pages long if I shared what is in my heart for each of you. I send all of you my love. My gratitude to you is immense for believing in my dream, supporting me, and encouraging me to tell my story

Abdoul Oubeidillah Abel
Gashe
Al Woudie
Alexis Tetreault
Allison Carpenter
Anand Daniel
Anteneh Girma
Asana Abu
Faheem Judah
Barbara Molo

Berhanu Teklemichael
Carita Myyrylainen
Charli Doll
Sudha Patel
Dawit Megistu
Deborah Vazirani
David Patterson
Eden Ayele
Elias Adan
Emebet Bekele

Emerntine Soulcie
Emma Day
Eskedar Yeshivas
Eskedar Sahilu
Esu Meaze
Evgenia Borisov
Eyerusalem Gedlu
Fahad Mir
Gabriel Negassa (family)
Gelila Tewolde
Girma Worku
Girma Tewolde
Gakig
Hamere Demissie
Hirut Wodajo
Haile Beyene (family)
Ioanna Margaroni
Isabelle Laporte
Jeanette Haenseroth
Jassica Levin
Jo Magpie
Katherine Peck
Katherine Karl
Katherine Sainty
Laurence Leigh
Lezka Rodr Ã-guez
Livingston Mukasa
Liben Eabisa
Menna Mennasemay
Marcelle Mondor
Marci Bravo
Martine Chaussard
Mesert Ayele
Oshi Mathur
Paolo Paliotti
Paul Lau
Praveen Reddy
Ralf Unterstab

Rebecca Haviv
Renee Stauffer
Reza Rashid
Robert Boardman
Roberto Corona
Saeed Sultan
Samson Kebede
Stéphane Thinel
Salahadin Khalifa
Sally DeHaven
Shoa Girma
Sirk Zena
Sofnias Nega
Temesgen Kabtyimer
Tesfa Michael Andemeskel
Thinat getu Alem
Timothee Labelle
Yodit Beyene
Yvette M Pennacchia
Yve Marion
Zaina Brown
Zaza Gomurashvili
Le Chalet d'en haut - Boys and Girls (you know who you are)

The **Couchsurfing community** around the world, and to **you readers**.